PROBABLE SONS.

BY

AMY LE FEUVRE

'A LITTLE CHILD SHALL LEAD THEM.'

Lamplighter Publishing
Waverly, PA 18471

The Lamplighter Rare Collector's Series is a series
of family Christian literature from the 17th, 18th, and
19th centuries. Each edition is printed in an attractive
hard-bound collector's format. For more information
call us toll-free at 1-888-246-7735, visit us at www.
lamplighterpublishing.com or write:

Lamplighter Publishing
P.O. Box 777
Waverly, PA 18471

Author: Amy LeFeuvre
Printed by Jostens in the United States of America
Cover: Cialux 1576 Rust, Crown Roll Leaf 11146, API
4039m Smooth Gold

ISBN 1-58474-033-7

PREFACE.

Maxwell Perkins, Scribner's editor, once wrote to Marjorie Rawlings, author of <u>The Yearling</u>, that, "Most of the best books in the world are read by both children and adults. This is a characteristic of a great book, that it is both juvenile and adult."

Believing this to be true, I would like to present to my readers a book that will be loved by all ages. <u>Probable Sons</u> not only possesses all of the characteristics of a Lamplighter Rare Collector book, but this book goes a step further; it delves into the heart issues of unforgiveness and reconciliation. In a world of broken relationships, our little heroine Milly will help us tear away the layers of stubbornness and pride and will provide a path that can help heal the most hurtful pain of the past.

The finding and publishing of these remarkable books is due to the blessing of a Father who delights in giving His children the desires of their hearts. "Father above, I dedicate this book to you with the hope that many a probable son will turn their hearts back home. May the truths found in this little story find a resting place in many hearts that have strayed so far from home. In the name of your Son Jesus, I thank you. Amen."

Mark Hamby
Luke 15:11-31

'Probable Sons'

CHAPTER I.

An Unwelcome Legacy.

CHILDREN! They are a nuisance to every one—my abomination, as you know, Jack. Why on earth they cannot be kept out of sight altogether till they reach a sensible age is what puzzles me! And I suppose if anything could make the matter worse, it is that this is a girl!'

The tone of disgust with which the last word was uttered brought a laugh from Sir Edward Wentworth's companion, who gazed critically into the worried, perplexed face of his host, and replied,–

'My dear fellow, she is not of an age yet to trouble you much. Wait till she gets a bit older; when her education is finished, and she takes possession of you and your house, will be the time for you to look to us for pity!' 'Look here, Sir Edward,' said a bright-looking youth from the other side of the room, 'I'll give you a bit of advice. Send the child straight off to school. Has she come to-day? Good. Then pack her off to-morrow, and keep her there as long as is needful. Then I will go down and inspect her, and if she grows up to be a moderately decent-looking girl, I will do you a good turn by taking her off your hands. She will have a nice little fortune, you informed us, and if you will give her something in addition, out of gratitude to me for relieving you of all responsibility concerning her, upon my word I think I should not do badly!'

But Sir Edward was not in a mood to joke; he looked gloomily round upon his friends, as they gathered round the fire after a hard day's shooting, and remarked,–

'I know what is before me. I have seen it in my sister's family, and have heard something of all her toils and troubles. How thankful I was when she and hers were translated to Australia, and the sea came between us! It is first the nurses, who run off and brings all kinds of followers about the house, who sometimes make off with one's plate. Then it's the governesses, who come and have a try at the guests, or most likely in my case they would set their affections on me, and get the reins of government entirely into their hands. If it is school, then there is a mass of correspondence about the child's health and training; and in addition, I shall have all the ladies in the neighbourhood coming to mother the child and tell me how to train it. It is a bad look-out for me, I can tell you, and not one of you would care to be in my shoes.'

'What is the trouble, Ned?' asked a new-comer, opening the door and glancing at the amused faces of those surrounding Sir Edward, all of whom seemed to be keenly enjoying their host's perplexity.

'He has received a legacy to-day, that is all,' was the response; 'he has had an orphan niece and nurse sent to him from some remote place in the Highlands. Come, give us your case again, old fellow, for the benefit of your cousin.'

Sir Edward, a grave, abstracted-looking man, with an iron-grey moustache and dark, piercing eyes, looked up with a desponding shake of the head, and repeated slowly and emphatically,–

'A widowed sister of mine died last year, and left her little girl in charge of an old school friend, who has now taken a husband to herself and discarded the child, calmly sending me the following letter:–

' " Dear Sir,

' " Doubtless you will remember that your sister's great desire on her death-bed was that you should receive her little one and bring her up under your own eye, being her natural guardian and nearest relative. Hearing, however, from you that you did not at that time feel equal to the responsibility, I came forward, and volunteered to take her for a short while till you had made arrangements to receive her. I have been expecting to hear from you for some time, and as I have promised my future husband to fix the day for our marriage some time early next month, I thought I could not do better than send the child with her nurse to you without delay. She will reach you the day after you receive this letter. Perhaps you will kindly send me word of her safe arrival.

'" Yours truly,

'" ANNA KENT."

'Now, Lovell, what do you think of that? And sure enough this afternoon, whilst we were out, the child and nurse appeared, and are in the house at this present moment. Don't you think it a hard case for such a confirmed bachelor as I am?'

'I do indeed,' was the hearty reply; 'but I think you will find a way out of it, Ned. Take a wife unto yourself, and she will relieve you of all responsibility.'

There was a general laugh at this, but in the midst of it the door slowly opened, and the subject of all this discussion appeared on the threshold, a fragile little figure, with long, golden-brown hair, and a pair of dark brown eyes that looked calmly and searchingly in front of her. Clad in white, with her dimpled hands crossed in front of her, she stood there for a moment in silence, then spoke:–

'Where is my Uncle Edward?'

'Here,' replied Sir Edward, as he looked helplessly round, first at his friends and then at his small niece.

The child stepped up to him with perfect composure, and held out her little hand, which her uncle took, undergoing all the while a severe scrutiny from the pair of dark eyes fixed upon him. There was dead silence in the room; Sir Edward's companions were delighting in the scene, and his great discomfiture only heightened their enjoyment.

'Well,' he said at length, rather feebly, 'I think you know the look of me now, don't you? Where is your nurse? Ought you not to be in your bed? This is not the place for little girls, you know.'

'I was thinking you would kiss me good night,' and the child's lips began to quiver, whilst a pink flush rose to her cheeks, and she glanced wistfully round, in the hope of seeing some sympathetic face near her.

But Sir Edward could not bring himself to do this; laying his hand on the curly head raised to his, he patted it as he might his dog, and said,–

'There, there! Now you have introduced yourself to me, you can run away. What is your name? Millicent, isn't it?'

'Milly is my name. And are all these gentlemen my uncles too?'

The tone of doubtful inquiry was too much for the little company, and Milly's question was answered by a shout of laughter.

Again the child's face flushed, and then a grey-haired man stepped forward.

'Come, Wentworth, this is a severe ordeal for such a mite. I have grandchildren of my own, so am not so scared as you. Now, little one, is that better?'

And in an instant the child was lifted by him and placed upon his knee as he took a seat by the fire.

Milly heaved a short sigh.

'I like this,' she said, looking up at him confidingly. 'Does Uncle Edward really want me to go to bed? Nurse said it wasn't time yet. Nurse wanted her supper, so she sent me in here while she had it.'

'The reign of the nurse has begun,' said Sir Edward. 'Well, it may be a very fine joke to all you fellows, but if I don't make my authority felt at once, it will be all up with me. Lovell, be so good as to ring that bell.'

Sir Edward's voice was irate when his old butler appeared.

'Ford, take this child to her nurse, and tell her that she is never to appear in my presence again unless sent for. Now, Millicent, go at once.'

The child slid down from her seat, but though evidently puzzled at the quick, sharp words, she seemed to have no fear, for, going up to her uncle, she slipped her little hand into his.

'Are you angry, uncle?   What does "presence" mean?   Will you say, "Good-night; God bless you," to me?'

With the baby fingers clinging to his, what could Sir Edward say?

'Good-night; good-night, child! Now go.'

'Say, "God bless you!" ' persisted the little one; and it was not till her uncle muttered the desired words that she relinquished her hold and followed the butler sedately out of the room.

CHAPTER II.

David and Goliath.

SIR EDWARD WENTWORTH was, as
he expressed it, a 'confirmed bachelor,'
and though during the autumn months
he was quite willing to fill his house with his
London friends, he was better pleased to live
the greater part of the year in seclusion,
occupying himself with looking after his
estate and writing articles for several of the
leading reviews of the day.

The advent of his small niece was indeed a
great trial to him, but, with his characteristic
thoroughness, he determined that he would
make the necessary arrangements for her
comfort. Accordingly he had a long interview

with her nurse the following morning. It
proved to be satisfactory. The nurse was a
staid, elderly woman, who assured him she
was accustomed to the sole charge of the
child, and would keep her entirely under her
own control.

'I expect you would like her to be sent down
to you in the evening—at dessert, perhaps,
sir?' she inquired.

Sir Edward pulled the ends of his moustache
dubiously. 'Is it necessary? I thought
children ought to be in bed at that time.'

'Of course it shall be as you like, sir. You
do not dine so late as some do. I thought you
would expect to see her once in the day.'

After a little hesitation Sir Edward gave his
permission; and when he found that Milly
neither screamed nor snatched for the fruit on
the table, and did not herself engross the
whole conversation, he became quite
reconciled to the little white figure stealing in
and occupying the chair that was always
placed at his left-hand side for her.

Beyond this he saw very little of her whilst
his guests were with him; but afterwards,

when they had all left him, and he relapsed
into his ordinary life, he was constantly
coming across her. Sometimes he would find
her in the stables, her arms round the stable
cat, and the grooms holding a voluble
conversation with her, or amongst the cows at
the bottom of the paddock, or feeding the pigs
and fowls in the poultry yard. Generally she
was attended by Fritz, a beautiful collie, who
had, with the fickleness of his nature,
transferred his affection from his master to
her, and though uncertain in temper towards
most, was never anything but amiable when
with the little girl.

Her uncle's form approaching was quite a
sufficient hint to her to make herself scarce;
she would generally anticipate the usual
formula: 'Now run away, child, to nurse,' by
singing out cheerfully; 'I am just off, uncle,'
and by the time he had reached the spot where
she had been standing the little figure would
be running off in the distance, Fritz close at
her heels.

One afternoon Sir Edward was returning
from a stroll up the avenue when he saw the

child at play amongst the trees, and for a
moment he paused and watched her.   She
appeared to be very busy with a doll wrapped
in a fur rug, which she carefully deposited at
the foot of a tree; then for some minutes she
and Fritz seemed to be having a kind of game
of hide-and-seek with one another, until she
pushed him into a bush and commanded him
to stay there.   Suddenly dog and child darted
at each other, and then, to Sir Edward's
amazement, he saw his little niece seize Fritz
by the throat and bring him to the ground.
When both were rolling over one another, and
Fritz's short, sharp barks became rather
indignant in tone, as he vainly tried to escape
from the little hands so tightly round him, Sir
Edward thought it high time to interfere.

'Millicent,' he called out sharply, 'come to
me at once: what are you doing?'

In an instant Milly was upon her feet, and
lifting a hot, flushed little face to his, she
placed herself in her favourite attitude when
in his presence: her hands clasped behind her
back, and feet closely planted together.
'Don't you know Fritz might bite if you are

so rough with him? Were you trying to choke
him?' demanded her uncle.

'Yes,' she responded, breathless from her
late exertions. 'I was trying to kill him! He's
a bear, and that's my lamb, and I am David;
that's all.'

A child's games were beyond Sir Edward's
comprehension. He looked down upon her
with a knitted brow.

She continued,–

'You see, he has to do for both, a bear and a
lion, for they both came, and they both tried
to get the lamb. Nurse was the lion one day,
but she is too big; I can't knock her down,
though I try hard.'

'I will not have Fritz knocked down in that
fashion; he might hurt you,' said Sir Edward
sternly.

Milly looked sorrowful; then brightening up,
she asked,–

'But I may kill Goliath, mayn't I? Do you
know, that is one of my games. See, I'm
David, and you see that big old tree standing
by itself? That's Goliath. He is looking at
me now. Do you see where his eyes come?

Just up there in those first branches. When it's windy he shakes his head at me fearful! He's a wicked, wicked old thing, and he thinks no one can knock him down. Do you remember about him, uncle?'

Sir Edward was becoming slightly interested. He leant against a tree and said,–

'No, I don't think I do.'

'Don't you remember? He stood up so proud, and called out: "Choose a man to come and fight me." He's saying that to me now. I'm David, you know, and I'm going. Just wait a moment till I'm ready.'

She darted away to where her doll was, and soon returned with a tiny calico bag, which she opened very carefully and disclosed to her uncle's puzzled gaze five round stones.

'You see,' she went on, 'it's a pity I haven't a sling, but Tom in the stable says he will make me a cattyput[1]; that's a lovely sling, he says, which would kill anything. But it's all right; I pretend I have a sling, you know. Now you wait here; I'm going to meet him.

---

[1] catapult

I'm not a bit afraid, though he looks so big, because David wasn't, you know. God helped him. Now, Goliath, I'm ready!'

Sir Edward looked on in some amusement, as Milly stepped out with regular, even steps until she was about twenty feet from the tree, then suddenly stopped.

'I hear what you say, Goliath. You say you'll give my body to be pecked at and eaten by the birds; but you won't do that, for I am coming, and I am going to kill you.'

And then with all her strength the child flung her stones one by one at the tree, pausing for some moments when she had done so.

'He's quite dead, uncle,' she said calmly, as she retraced her steps and stood before Sir Edward, again looking up at him with those earnest eyes of hers, 'quite dead; and if I had a sword I would play at cutting off his head. I suppose you wouldn't lend me your sword hanging up in the hall, would you?'

' Most certainly not,' was the quick reply; then Sir Edward asked: 'And does all your play consist in killing people?'

'I only try to kill the bear and lion and Goliath, because they're so wicked and so strong.'

Milly continued,–

'This is such a lovely place to play in–trees are so nice to have games with. Shall I tell you some more? You see that little tree over there? That's where I sit when I'm the probable son, and when I've sat there a long time and been very miserable, and eaten some of the beech nuts that do for husks, then suddenly I think I will go home to my father. It's rather a long walk, but I get happier and happier as I go, and I get to walk very quick at last, and then I run when I see my father. Do you see that nice big old tree right up there with the red leaves, uncle? That's him, and I run up and say, "Father, I have sinned; I am not fit to come back, but I am so sorry that I left you," and then I just hug him and kiss him; and, do you know, I feel he hugs and kisses me back. He does in the story, you know. And then I have a nice little feast all ready: I get some biscuits from nurse, and a little jam, and some sugar and water, and I sit down and feel so happy to think I'm not the probable son any more, and haven't got to eat husks or be with the pigs. Don't you think that's a beautiful game, uncle?'

'Do you get all your games from the Bible?' inquired Sir Edward. 'I somehow think it is not quite correct,' and he looked very dubiously at his little niece as he spoke.

'Well,' said Milly, the earnest look coming into her eyes again, 'I love the Bible so much, you see. Nurse tells me the stories ever so often, and I know lots and lots of them. But I like the probable son quite the best. Do you like it?'

Sir Edward strolled on without a reply. His little niece's words awakened very uncomfortable feelings within his heart. Years before he had known and loved his Bible well. He had been active in Christian work, and had borne many a scoff and jeer from his companions when at Oxford for being 'pious,' as they termed it. But there came a time when coldness crept into his Christianity, and worldly ambition and desires filled his soul; gradually he wandered farther and farther from the right path, and when he came into his property he took possession of it with no other aim and object in life than to enjoy himself in his own way, and to totally ignore both the past and future. Beyond going to church once on Sunday he made no profession of religion, but that custom he conformed to most regularly, and the vicar of the parish had nothing to complain of in the way in which his appeals for charity were met by the squire.

It is needless to say that Sir Edward was not a happy man; there were times when he could not bear his own thoughts and the solitude of his position, and at such times there was a hasty departure for town, and some weeks of club life ensued, after which he would return to his home, and engross himself in both his literary and country occupations with fresh vigor.

CHAPTER III.

The First Punishment.

SLOWLY but surely little Milly was advancing in her uncle's favour. Her extreme docility and great fearlessness, added to her quaintness of speech and action, attracted him greatly. He became interested in watching her little figure as it flitted to and fro, and the sunny laugh and bright childish voice about the house were no longer an annoyance to him.

One day he was moved to anger by an accident that happened to a small statue in the hall, and Milly was the delinquent. Her ball had rolled behind it, and both she and the dog were having a romp to get it, when in the scuffle the statue came to the ground and lay there in a thousand pieces. Hearing the crash, Sir Edward came out of his study, and completely losing his temper, he turned furiously upon the child, giving vent to language that was hardly fit for her ears to hear. She stood before him with round, frightened eyes and quivering lips, her little figure upright and still, until she could bear it no longer; and then she turned and fled from him through the garden door out upon the smooth grassy lawn, where she flung herself down on her face close to her favourite beech-tree, there giving way to a burst of passionate tears.

'I didn't mean it—oh! I didn't mean to break it!' she sobbed aloud. 'Uncle Edward is a fearful angry man; he doesn't love me a bit. I wish I had a father! I want a father, like the probable son; he wouldn't be so angry!'

And when later on nurse came, with an anxious face, to fetch her little charge in from the cold, wet grass, she had not the heart to scold her, for the tear-stained face was raised so pitifully to hers, with the words,—

'Oh, nurse, dear, carry me in your arms. No one loves me here. I've been telling God all about it. He's the only One that isn't angry.'

That evening, at the accustomed time, Milly stole quietly into the dining-room, wondering in her little heart whether her uncle was still angry with her.

As she climbed into her chair, now placed on the opposite side of the large table, she eyed him doubtfully through her long eyelashes; then gathering courage from the immovable expression of his face, she said in her most cheerful tone,–

'It's a very fine night, uncle.'

'Is it?' responded Sir Edward, who was accustomed by this time to some such remark when his little niece wanted to attract his notice. Then feeling really ashamed of his outburst a few hours before, he said, by way of excusing himself,–

'Look here, Millicent, you made me exceedingly angry by your piece of mischief this afternoon. That statue can never be replaced, and you have destroyed one of my most valuable possessions. Let it be a warning for the future. If ever you break anything again, I shall punish you most severely; do you understand?'

'Yes, uncle,' she answered, looking up earnestly.   ' "You will punish me *most* severely." I will remember. I have been wondering why I broke it, when I didn't mean to do it. Nurse says it was a most "unfortunate accident." I asked her what an accident was. She says it's a thing that happens when you don't expect it–a surprise, she called it. I'm sure it was a dreadful surprise to me, and to Fritz too; but I'll never play ball in the hall again, *never*!'

A week later, and Sir Edward was in his study, absorbed in his books and papers, when there was a knock at his door, and, to his astonishment, his little niece walked in. This was so against all rules and regulations that his voice was very stern as he said,–

'What is the meaning of this intrusion, Millicent? You know you are never allowed to disturb me when here.'

Milly did not answer for a moment; she walked up to her uncle, her small lips tightly closed, and then, standing in front of him with clasped hands, she said,–

'I've come to tell you some dreadful news.'

Sir Edward pushed aside his papers, adjusted his glasses, and saw from the pallor of the child's face and the scared expression in her eyes, that it was no light matter that had made her venture into his presence uncalled for.

'It's a dreadful surprise again,' Milly continued, 'but I told nurse I must tell you at once. I—I felt so bad here,' and her little hand was laid pathetically on her chest.

'Well, what is it? Out with it, child! You are wasting my time,' said her uncle impatiently.

'I have—I have broken something else.'

There was silence. Then Sir Edward asked drily,–

'And what is it now?'

'It's a—a flower-pot, that the gardener's boy left outside the tool-house. I—I—well, I put it on Fritz's head for a hat, you know. He did look so funny, but he tossed up his head and ran away, and it fell, and it is smashed to bits.

I have got the bits outside the door on the mat. Shall I bring them in?'

A flower-pot was of such small value in Sir Edward's eyes that he almost smiled at the child's distress.

'Well, well, you must learn not to touch the flower-pots in future; now run away, and do not disturb me again.'

But Milly stood her ground.

'I think you have forgot, Uncle Edward. You told me that if I broke anything again you would punish me *"most severely."* Those were the words you said; don't you remember?'

Sir Edward pulled the ends of his moustache and fidgeted uneasily in his chair. He always prided himself upon being a man of his word, but much regretted at the present moment that he had been so rash in his speech.

'Oh! ah! I remember,' he said at length, meeting his little niece's anxious gaze with some embarrassment. Then, pulling himself together, he added sternly,–

'Of course you must be punished; it was exceedingly careless and mischievous. What does your nurse do when she punishes you?'

'She never does punish me—not now,' said Milly plaintively. 'When I was very little girl I used to stand in the corner. I don't think nurse has punished me for years.'

Sir Edward was in a dilemma: children's punishments were quite unknown to him. Milly seemed to guess at his difficulty.

'How were you punished when you were a little boy, uncle?'

'I used to be well thrashed. Many is the whipping that I have had from my father!'

'What is a whipping—like you gave Fritz when he went into the game wood?'

'Yes.'

There was a pause. The child clasped her little hands tighter and set her lips firmer, as she saw before her eyes a strong arm dealing very heavy strokes with a riding-whip. Then she said in an awe-struck tone,–

'And do you think that is how you had better punish me?'

Sir Edward smiled grimly as he looked at the baby figure standing so erect before him.

'No,' he said; 'I do not think you are a fit subject for that kind of treatment.'

Milly heaved a sigh of relief.

'And don't you know how to punish?' she said, after some minutes of awkward silence. There was commiseration in her tone. The situation was becoming ludicrous to Sir Edward, though there was a certain amount of annoyance at feeling his inability to carry out his threat.

'Nurse told me,' continued his little niece gravely, 'that she skew a little boy who was shut up in a dark cupboard for a punishment; but he was found nearly dead, and really died the next day, from fright. There is a dark cupboard on the kitchen stairs; I don't think I should be very frightened, because God will be in there with me. Do you think that would do?'

This was not acceptable. The child went on, with knitted brows; 'I expect the Bible will tell you how to punish. I remember a man who picked up sticks on Sunday: he was stoned dead; and Elisha's servant was made a leper, and some children were killed by a bear, and a prophet by a lion, and Annas and Sophia were struck dead. All of them were punished "most severely," weren't they? If you forgave me a little bit, and left out the "most severely," it would make it easier, I expect.'

'Perhaps I might do that,' said poor Sir Edward, who by this time longed to dispense with the punishment altogether; 'as it was only a flower-pot, I will leave out the "most severely."'

Milly's face brightened.

'I think,' she said, coming up to him and laying one hand on his knee—'I think if I were to go to bed instead of coming down to dessert with you this evening, that would punish me; don't you think so?'

'Very well, that will do. Now run away, and let this be your last breakage. I cannot be worried with your punishments.'

'I will try to be very good, nurse, always,' said Milly, whilst being tucked up in bed that night, 'because Uncle Edward is very puzzled when he has to punish me. He doesn't know what to do. He looked quite unhappy, and said it worried him.'

And Sir Edward as he finished his dinner in silence and solitude muttered to himself,–

'That child is certainly a great nuisance at times, but, upon my word, I quite miss her this evening. Children after all are original, if they are nothing else, and she is one of the most original that I have ever met.'

It was Sunday morning, and Sir Edward was just starting for church. As he stood over the blazing fire in the hall buttoning a glove, a little voice came to him from the staircase,–

'Uncle Edward, may I come down and speak to you?'

Permission being given, Milly danced down the stairs, and then, slipping her little hand into her uncle's, she lifted a coaxing face to his.

'Will you take me to church with you? Nurse thinks I'm almost big enough now, and I have been to church in the afternoon sometimes.'

Sir Edward hesitated.

'If you come, you will fidget, I expect. I cannot stand that.'

'I will sit as still as a mouse; I won't fidget.'

'If you behave badly, I shall never take you again. Yes, you may come; be quick and get ready.'

A few moments after, Sir Edward and his little niece were walking down the avenue, she clasping a large Bible under her arm, and trying in vain to match her steps with his.

The squire's pew was one of the old-fashioned high ones, and Milly's head did not reach the top of it. Very quiet and silent she was during the service, and very particular to follow her uncle's example in every respect, though she nearly upset his gravity at the outset by taking off her hat in imitation of him, and covering her face with it. But when the sermon commenced her large dark eyes were riveted on the clergyman, as he gave out the text so well known to her:

'I will arise and go to my father, and will say unto him, Father I have sinned against Heaven, and before thee, and am no more worthy to be called thy son:' and though the sermon was half an hour in length, her gaze never left the pulpit.

'Uncle Edward,' she said, when their steps at length turned homewards, 'do you know, I heard all the sermon, and understood it pretty well except the long words. Wasn't it nice to hear about the probable son?'

' "Prodigal," you mean; cannot you pronounce your words properly?'

Sir Edward's tone was irritable. He had not been feeling very comfortable under the good vicar's words.

'I can't say that; I always forget it. Nurse says one long word is as good as another sometimes. Uncle, what did the clergyman mean by people running away from God? No one does, do they?'

'A great many do,' was the dry response.

'But how can they? Because God is everywhere. No one can't get away from God, and why do they want to? Because God loves them so.'

'Why did the prodigal want to get away?'

Milly considered.

'I s'pose he wanted to have some a–
aventures, don't you call them? I play at that,
you know. All sorts of things happen to me
before I sit down at the beech-tree, but–but
it's so different with God. Why, I should be
fearful unhappy if I got away from Him. I
couldn't, could I, uncle? Who would take
care of me and love me when I'm asleep?
And who would listen to my prayers? Why,
Uncle Edward, I think I should die of fright if
I got away from God. Do tell me I couldn't.'

Milly had stopped short, and grasped hold of
Sir Edward's coat in her growing excitement.
He glanced at her flushed cheeks and
sparkling eyes.

'You foolish child, there is no fear of your
getting away from God. Don't be so
excitable. We will change the subject. I want
to see Maxwell, so we will go through the
wood.

Maxwell was Sir Edward's head keeper, and
a little later found them at his pretty cottage at
the edge of the wood. It was Milly's first
visit, and Mrs. Maxwell, a motherly-looking

body, greeted her with such a sunshiny smile that the child drew near to her instinctively.

'What a lovely room!' she exclaimed, looking round the homely little kitchen with a child's admiring eyes, 'and what a beautiful cat! May I stroke her?'

Assent being given, Milly was soon seated in a large cushioned chair, a fat tabby cat on her lap, and whilst Sir Edward was occupied with his keeper, she was making fast friends with the wife.

'Uncle Edward,' she said, when they had taken their leave and were walking homewards, 'Mrs. Maxwell has asked me to go to tea with her to-morrow. May I–all by myself?'

'Ask your nurse; I have no objection.'

'I should love to live in her house,' continued the child eagerly; 'it is all amongst the trees, and I love them. And this wood is so lovely. Why, I might get lost in it, mightn't I? I have never been here before. In my story-books, children always get lost in a wood. Uncle Edward, do you think the trees talk to one another? I always think they do.

Look at them now. They are just shaking their heads together and whispering, aren't they? Whispering very gently to-day, because it is Sunday. Sometimes they get angry with one another and scream, but I like to hear them hum and sing best. Nurse says it's the wind that makes them do it. Don't you like to hear them? When I lie in bed I listen to them round the house, and I always want to sing with them. Nurse doesn't like it; she says it's the wind moaning: I think it's the trees singing to God, and I love them when they do it. Which do you think it is?'

And so Milly chatted on, and Sir Edward listened, and put in a word or two occasionally, and on the whole did not find his small niece bad company. He told her when they entered the house that she could go to church every Sunday morning in future with him, and that sent Milly to the nursery with a radiant face, there to confide to nurse that she had had a 'lovely time,' and was going to tea as often as she might with 'Mrs. Maxwell in the wood.'

CHAPTER IV.

Mrs. Maxwell's Sorrow.

MILLY spent a very happy afternoon at the keeper's cottage the next day, and came down to dessert in the evening so full of her visit that she could talk of nothing else.

'They were so kind to me, uncle. Mrs. Maxwell made a hot currant cake on purpose for me, and the cat had a red ribbon for company, and we sat by the fire and talked when Maxwell was out, and she told me such lovely stories, and I saw a beautiful picture of the Probable Son in the best parlour, and Mrs. Maxwell took it down and let me have a good look at it. I am going to save up my money and buy one just like it for my nursery, and do you know, uncle—'

She stopped short, but not for want of breath. Putting her curly head on one side, she surveyed her uncle for a minute meditatively, then asked a little doubtfully: —

'Can you keep a secret, Uncle Edward? Because I would like to tell you, only, you see, Mrs. Maxwell doesn't talk about it, and I told her I wouldn't—at least not to the servants, you know.'

'I think you can trust me,' Sir Edward said gravely.

'This is it, then, and I think it's so wonderful. They have got a real live probable son.'

Sir Edward raised his eyebrows. His little niece continued,—

'Yes, they really have. It was when I was talking about the picture Mrs. Maxwell took the corner of her apron and wiped her eyes, and said she had a dear son who had run away from home, and she hadn't seen him for nine years. Just fancy! Where was I nine years ago?'

'Not born.'

'But I must have been somewhere,' and Milly's active little brain now started another train of thought, until she got fairly bewildered.

'I expect I was fast asleep in God's arms,' she said at length, with knitted brows, 'only of course I don't remember;' and having settled that point to her satisfaction, she continued her story: —

'Mrs. Maxwell's probable son is called Tommy. He ran away when he was seventeen, because he didn't like the blacksmith's shop—Mrs. Maxwell and I cried about him—he had such curly hair and stood six feet in his stockings, and he was a *beautiful* baby when he was little, and had croup and—and confusions, and didn't come to for four hours, but he would run away, though he laid the fire and put sticks on it, and drew the water for Mrs. Maxwell before he went. And Mrs. Maxwell says he may be a soldier now for all she knows, and he may be drowned dead, or run over, or have both his legs shot to pieces, or he may be in India; but

I told her he was very likely taking care of some pigs somewhere, and she got happy a little bit then, and we dried our tears, and she gave me some peppermint to suck. Isn't it a wonderful story, uncle?'

'Very wonderful,' was the response.

'Well, we were in the middle of talking when Maxwell came in, so we hushed, because Mrs. Maxwell said, "It makes my man so sad;" but, do you know, when Maxwell was bringing me home through the wood he asked me what we had been talking about, and he said he knew it was about the boy, because he could see it in Mrs. Maxwell's eye. And then I asked him if he would run and kiss Tommy when he came back, and if he would make a feast; and he said he would do anything to get him home again.'

Milly paused, then said wistfully,—

'I wish I had a father, Uncle Edward. You see, nurse does for a mother, but fathers are so fond of their children, aren't they?'

'It does not always follow that they are,' Sir Edward replied.

'The probable son's father loved him, and Maxwell loves Tommy, and then there was David, you know, who really had a wicked son, with long hair—I forget his name—and he cried dreadful when he was dead. I sometimes tell God about it when I'm in bed, and then He–he just seems to put Him arms round me and send me off to sleep; at least, I think He does. Nurse says God likes me to call Him my Father, but of course that isn't quite the same as having a father I can see. Maxwell is a very nice father, I think. I told him I would pray for Tommy every night when I go to bed, and then I told him that God had lots of probable sons, too–the clergyman said so on Sunday, didn't he?— people who have run away from Him. I've been asking God to make them come back. I hope He will let me know when they do. Do you know any one who has run away from God, uncle?'

'You are chattering too much, child,' said Sir Edward irritably; 'sit still and be quiet.'

Milly instantly obeyed, and after some moments of silence her uncle said,—

'I don't mind your going to Maxwell's cottage, but you must never take Fritz with you. He is not allowed in that wood at all. Do you quite understand?'

'Yes, but I'm very sorry, for Fritz doesn't like being left behind; the tears were in his eyes when nurse told him he wasn't to go with me. You see, no one talks to him like I do. He likes me to tell him stories, and I told him when I came back about my visit, so he wants to go. But I won't take him with me if you say no.'

When she was leaving Sir Edward that night for bed, she paused a moment as she wished him good-night.

'Uncle Edward, when you say your prayers to-night, will you ask God to make Tommy come back home? His mother does want him so badly.'

'I will leave you to do that,' was the curt reply.

'Well, if you don't want to pray for Tommy, pray for God's probable sons, won't you? Do, Uncle Edward. Mrs. Maxwell said the only thing that comforted her was asking God to bring Tommy back.'

Sir Edward made no reply, only dismissed her more peremptorily than usual, and when she had left the room he leaned his arms on the chimney-piece, and resting his head on them, gazed silently into the fire with a knitted brow. His thoughts did not soothe him, for he presently raised his head with a short laugh, saying to himself,—

'I shall have to curb that child's tongue a little; she is getting too troublesome.'

And whilst he was pacing moodily up and down the terrace outside, a little white-robed figure, with bent head and closed eyes, was saying softly and reverently, as she knelt at her nurse's knee: —

'And, O God, bring Tommy back, and don't let him be a probable son any more; bring him home very soon, please, and will You bring back all Your probable sons who are running away from You, for Jesus Christ's sake. Amen.'

Sir Edward did not escape several visits from ladies in the neighbourhood offering to befriend his little niece, but all these overtures were courteously and firmly rejected. He told them the child was happy with her nurse, he did not wish her to mix with other children at present, and a year or two hence would be quite time enough to think about her education. So Milly was left alone, more than one mother remarking with a shake of the head,—

'It's a sad life for a child, but Sir Edward is peculiar, and when he gets a notion into his head he keeps to it.'

The child was not unhappy, and when the days grew shorter, and her rambles out of doors were curtailed, she would lie on the tiger-skin by the hall fire with Fritz for the hour together, pouring to him all her childish confidences.

Sometimes her uncle would find her perched on the broad window-seat half-way up the staircase, with her little face pressed against the window-panes, and late on one very cold afternoon in November he remonstrated with her.

'It is too cold for you here, Millicent,' he said sternly; 'you ought to be in the nursery.'

'I don't feel cold,' she replied. 'I don't like being in the nursery all day; and when it gets dark, nurse will have the lamp lit and the curtains drawn, and then there are only the walls and ceiling and the pictures to look at. I'm tired of them; I see them every day.'

'And what do you see here?' asked Sir Edward.

'You come and sit down, and I will tell you. There's room, uncle; make Fritz move a little. Now, you look out with me. I can see such a lot from this window. I like looking out right into the world; don't you?'

'Are we not in the world? I thought we were.'

'I s'pose we are, but I mean God's world. The insides of houses aren't His world, are they? Do you see my trees? I can see Goliath from this window; he looks very fierce to-night; he has lost all his leaves, and I can almost hear him muttering to himself. And then, uncle, do you see those nice thin trees cuddling each other? I call those David and

Jon'than; they're just kissing each other, like they did in the wood, you know. Do you remember? And there's my beech-tree over there, where I sit when I'm the probable son. It's too dark for you to see all the others. I have names for them all nearly, but I like to come and watch them, and then I see the stars just beginning to come out. Do you know what I think about the stars? They're angels' eyes, and they look down and blink at me so kindly, and then I look up and blink back. We go on blinking at each other sometimes till I get quite sleepy. I watch the birds going to bed too. There is so much I can see from this window.'

'Well, run along to the nursery now; you have been here long enough.'

Milly jumped down from her seat obediently; then catching hold of her uncle's hand as he was moving away, she said,—

'Just one thing more I want to show you, uncle. I can see the high-road for such a long way over there, and when it is not quite so dark I sit and watch for Tommy—that's Maxwell's probable son, you know. I should

be so glad if I were to see him coming along
one day with his head hanging down, and all
ragged and torn. He is sure to come some
day—God will bring him—and if I see him
coming first, I shall run off quick to Maxwell
and tell him, and then he will run out to meet
him. Won't it be lovely?'

And with shining eyes Milly shook back her
brown curls and looked up into her uncle's
face for sympathy. He patted her head, the
nearest approach to a caress that he ever gave
her, and left her without saying a word.

Another day, later still, he came upon her at
the staircase window; he was dining out that
night, and was just leaving the house, but
stopped as he noticed his little niece earnestly
waving her handkerchief up at the window.

'What are you doing now?' he inquired as
he passed down the stairs. Milly turned
round, her little face flushed, and her eyes
looking very sweet and serious.

'I was just waving to God, Uncle Edward. I
thought I saw Him looking down at me from
the sky.'

Sir   Edward   passed   on,   muttering
inaudibly—

'I believe that child lives in the presence of
God from morning to night.'

'I WAS JUST WAVING TO GOD, UNCLE EDWARD.'

CHAPTER V.

A Prodigal.

'UNCLE EDWARD, nurse and I are going shopping: would you like us to buy you anything? We are going in the dog-cart with Harris.'

Milly was dancing up and down on the rug inside the front door as she spoke. It was a bright, frosty morning, and Sir Edward was leaving the breakfast-room with the newspaper and a large packet of letters in his hand. He stopped and glanced at the little fur-clad figure as she stood there, eager anticipation written on her face, and his thoughts went back to the time when he as a boy looked upon a day's visit to the neighbouring town–nine miles away–as one of his greatest pleasures.

'Yes,' he said, slowly fumbling in his waistcoat pocket; 'you can get me some pens and blotting-paper at the stationer's. I will write down the kind I want, and here is the money. Keep the change, and buy anything you like with it.'

He handed her half a sovereign, and Milly's cheeks flushed with delight as she took it.

'I've never had a gold piece of money before. What a lot it will buy!' she said. 'Thank you very much indeed. I was wanting to buy something my own self, and I've only a three-penny bit cook gave me, but now I shall be quite rich.'

It was late in the afternoon when nurse and her little charge drove back, and Sir Edward met them coming up the avenue. Milly's face was clouded, and there were traces of tears on her cheeks, and this was such an unusual sight that Sir Edward inquired of the nurse what was the matter.

'She has not been good, sir, I am sorry to say. It isn't often that I have to pull her up, but she has given me such a fright and trouble this afternoon as I am not likely to forget in a hurry.'

'What has she been doing? But never mind; I will not detain you now. I can hear about it when we get in.'

Nurse was evidently very disturbed in mind, for she poured into Sir Edward's ear, directly they were inside the hall, a confused story: —

'I was in the grocer's, sir, and I knew I should be there some time; for cook, she gave me so many commissions I had to write a long list of them. I said to Miss Milly, "You can stand outside, but don't go a step farther." She knows she is never allowed to speak to such people; I've known, as I told her, of children being carried bodily off and set down at a street corner with hardly a rag on their backs; and to think of her marching off with him, and never a thought of my anxiety–and the way I went rushing up and down the streets—and the policemen—they are perfectly useless to help a person, but can only stare at you and grin. I'm sure I never expected to light eyes on her again, and I lost my purse and my best umbrella; I left them both somewhere, but it was nigh on two hours I spent, and my shopping not near done, and he the greatest-looking rascal that one might see coming out of gaol. I'm sure I shouldn't have been so angry, but to see her smiling face, as if she hadn't done any wrong at all, nor disobeyed me flatly, and most likely put herself in the way of catching the most infectious disease from the very look of him, and run the risk of being robbed and perhaps murdered, and not an idea in her head that she was a very naughty child, but quite expected me to see the reasonableness of it all!'

Nurse stopped for breath, whilst Milly's hanging head, heaving chest, and quick sobs showed that by this time nurse's words had quite convinced her of her wrong-doing.

Sir Edward was surprised at the interest he felt in his little niece's trouble.

'I am afraid I cannot understand your story, nurse,' he said quietly; 'but I daresay Miss Millicent will tell me herself. Come into the study, child, with me.'

He took her hand in his, and led her away, whilst nurse looked after him in astonishment, and Ford, the old butler, standing by, said with great solemnity,—

'You may well stare, nurse. Mark my words, that child will be able to twist him round with her little finger one of these days. I see it a-developin'; it will be a terrible come-down to the master—but there, I will say that the women always conquer, and they begin it when they're in short frocks.'

'I don't see the remarkableness in a gentleman taking notice of his own sister's child,' returned nurse testily; 'the wonder is that he should hold her at arm's length as he does, and treat her as if she were a dog or a piece of furniture, without any feelings, and she his own flesh and blood, too. There's no "coming down" to have a spark of humanity in his breast occasionally.' And nurse sailed upstairs, the loss of her purse and umbrella having considerably ruffled her usually even temper.

Sir Edward seated himself by the study fire, and Milly stood before him, one little hand resting upon his knee and the other holding her tiny handkerchief to her eyes, and vainly trying to restrain her sobs.

'Now suppose you stop crying, and tell me what has happened!' her uncle said, feeling moved at seeing his usually self-contained little niece in such grief.

Milly applied her handkerchief vigorously to her eyes, and looking up with quivering lips, she said,—

'I didn't mean to be naughty, uncle, Nurse hasn't been angry with me like she is now for *years*, and I'm *so* unhappy!'

The pitiful tone and look touched Sir Edward's heart, and, on the impulse of the moment, he did what he had never as yet attempted: lifted her upon his knee, and told her to proceed with her story; and Milly, after a final struggle with her tears, got the better of them, and was able to give him a pretty clear account of what had happened.

'I had bought you pens and blotting-paper, uncle, and was going to a picture-shop to spend the rest of my money when nurse had finished at the grocer's. I was standing outside, when I saw a man coming along. He limped, and his hat was broken in, and he was so ragged that I thought he must be a probable son, and then I thought he might be Tommy going home; and when I thought that, I couldn't think of anything else, and I forgot all about nurse, and I forgot she told me to stay there, and I ran after him as hard as I could. I caught him up, and he looked very astonished when I asked him was his name Tommy. He said "No," and he laughed at me, and then I asked him was he a probable son, because he looked like one. He said he didn't know what kind of person that was. And then I had to explain it to him. He told me he had never had a home to run away from, so that wouldn't do; but he really looked just like the man I've seen in Mr. Maxwell's picture, and I told him so, and then I found out what he was, and I was so sorry, and yet I was so glad.'

Milly paused, and her large, expressive eyes shone as she turned them up to her uncle's face, and her voice dropped almost to a whisper as she said,—

'I found out he was one of God's probable sons. When I asked him if he had run away from God, he said yes, he supposed he had done that, so of course he was ragged and unhappy.'

'That is not always the case,' put in Sir Edward, half touched, half amused. 'Sometimes it is very rich people who run away from God, and they get richer when they are away from Him.'

Milly looked puzzled.

'But they can't be happy, uncle. Oh, they never can be!'

'Perhaps not.'

'Well, I talked to this poor man till we had walked quite away from the shops, and then he turned down a lane, and I went with him; and we were both rather tired, so we sat down together on some doorsteps inside an archway, and he told me all about himself. His name is Jack, and his father and mother are dead, like mine; and he got drunk one night, and fell down and broke his arm, and then he went to a hospital; and when he got well and went back to his work again, his master couldn't take him, because some one else was in his place, and he couldn't get any work. I asked him were there no pigs to keep, but he said there weren't any in London, and he was there, and for six months, he told me, he had been "on the tramp;" that's what he called it. I asked him what that meant, and he said just walking on every day to no place particular. And he said something about going to the bad, which I couldn't quite understand. Then I asked him why he didn't go back to God, and he said he had been a good boy once, when he went to Sunday-school, and he had a very good uncle who kept a baker's shop in London, and who wanted him to go and live with him, but he wouldn't, because he was too good for him. And I asked him why he wouldn't go to him now, and he said he couldn't tramp back again to London, it was too far, and he had no money. So then I opened my purse, and we counted over my money together, and he said it was seven shillings and a sixpence, and it would be just enough to take him back, if I would lend it to him. So of course I did, and he asked me my name and where I lived, and I told him.'

'The scoundrel!' muttered Sir Edward.

Milly paused. 'Why are you looking so angry, uncle? I was so glad to give him the money; and then we talked a good deal, and I begged him not to be one of God's probable sons any more. Fancy! He wouldn't believe God loved him, and he wouldn't believe that God wanted him back! I told him I should be quite frightened to get away from God, and he—well, he almost didn't seem to care; he said no one cared what came of him, whether he was hung dead, or not; and I told him no one cared for me much except nurse, but God did. I feel He loves me, and I know He loves Jack just the same; doesn't He, uncle?'

'And when did nurse find you?' inquired Sir Edward, evading this question.

Milly's little face, which had been gradually brightening with the interest of her story, now clouded over again, and she hung her head.

'She was fearful angry with me; she was quite hot and red, and she snatched me away, and said that Jack was a thief and—and a vagbag, or something like that. She scolded me all the way home, and I don't think she will ever love me again. She said it was just a chance she found me, and if she hadn't come along that lane I should have been lost for ever! And she was angry most of all because I shook hands with Jack and wished him goodbye. I don't think nurse would run and meet a probable son if she had one; she thinks all ragged people are wicked. But I'm—I'm dreadful sorry I was disobedient. Do you think I have been very naughty, Uncle Edward?'

Sir Edward twisted the ends of his moustache slowly. 'I think you were naughty to run after a strange man like that, and I quite understand nurse's displeasure. You made her exceedingly anxious.'

'And is God very angry with me?'

'God is not pleased with disobedient children.'

'May I kneel down and ask Him to forgive me now?'

Sir Edward hesitated.

'I think you had better go to the nursery and do it there.'

'I don't want to see nurse till I have done it. May I? Will you ask God to forgive me too?'

'Your prayer will be quite sufficient.'

Milly slipped off his knee, and then, kneeling down with folded hands and closed eyes, she said softly,—

'Please, God, will You forgive me? I'm so sorry I disobeyed nurse and ran away. And please take care of Jack, and bring him back to You, for Jesus Christ's sake. Amen.'

'Now run along to nurse, and don't cry any more,' said Sir Edward, as he rose from his seat.

Milly looked back wistfully as she reached the door.

'Do you think nurse is still angry?'

'Tell nurse from me that she need not scold you any more; the loss of your money ought to be a lesson to you.'

'But I didn't lose it, uncle; I lent it to Jack; he wouldn't let me give it to him; he said he would send it back to me in a letter.'

Sir Edward laughed unbelievingly, and Milly trotted upstairs, to be received with open arms by nurse at the nursery door.

'There! never mind, my dear. I have been very angry with you, but you'll never do such a thing again. Come and have your tea. I've had a cup already, and feel wonderful better. Now, don't cry any more: bless your little heart, I can't bear to see you in tears.'

With that nurse took her up in her arms; and poor, tired little Milly whispered as she clung to her,—

'I was afraid you would never love me again. I've told God I'm sorry; do you quite forgive me?'

'Quite, my lamb,' was the reply; 'and as to loving you, I shouldn't give over doing that if you were twice as troublesome.'

CHAPTER VI.

A Promise Kept.

ABOUT a fortnight later Sir Edward, who always opened the post-bag himself, found there a letter addressed to his little niece, and sent a message to the nursery to tell her to come down to him. She arrived very much surprised at the summons, as Sir Edward always wished to be left undisturbed at his breakfast; but when she saw the letters on the table she cried out joyously,–

'Good morning, Uncle Edward. I know there's a letter from Jack for me, isn't there? I've been waiting for it every day.'

'I think there may be, judging from the writing on the envelope. Come here and open it.'

Milly took the letter, and her little fingers fairly trembled with excitement as she opened it, saying softly to herself as she did so,—

'I knew he would keep his promise. I knew he wasn't a thief.'

A postal order for seven shillings and sixpence dropped out.

'Well,' said Sir Edward, 'you were right, little woman, and we were wrong. Would you like me to read it for you?'

'Yes, please, uncle.'

The letter read as follows:—

'I am as good as my word, little miss, in sending you back what you lent me with many grateful thanks for the loan, as I reached London safe and have never touched a drop of drink since I seen you, and am in work at my uncle's which is good of him to take me, and am getting twelve shillings a week and goes to church again. And my uncle has a chum which is a street preacher, and comes along of

plenty of fellows like I was, and I told him of
your young fellow, Tommy Maxwell, and he
will keep a look-out for him. Tell the woman
that fetched you sharp away that I'll hold up
my head with her yet, and every night I asks
God to bless you, for I hopes I am getting on
the right track again, and thank you kindly for
your talk, which is sticking to me.

> 'Yours obediently,
> 'Jack Gray'

Sir Edward laid the letter down in silence
when he had finished reading it. Milly's face
was radiant.

'I've never had a letter in my life before,
uncle, but I don't quite understand all of it.
Will you explain it to me?'

And this her uncle did, sending her upstairs
at length to show it to nurse, but sitting
wrapped in thought himself and leaving both
his letters and breakfast untouched for some
considerable time.

That same day he went out driving in the
afternoon with a young horse, and returning

home met a traction engine, at which the
horse instantly took fright and bolted.

For some time Sir Edward kept steadily to
his seat, and though powerless to check the
animal's course, was able to guide it; but in
spite of all his efforts the trap was at last
upset, and he was thrown violently to the
ground. He had no groom with him, and the
accident took place on a lonely road, so that it
was not till an hour later that help came in the
shape of a farmer returning from market in
his cart. He found Sir Edward unconscious,
and the horse still feebly struggling to
extricate himself from under the trap, which
was badly broken.

It was about seven o'clock in the evening
when Sir Edward was brought home, and he
had three ribs broken, besides some very
severe injuries to his head. The doctor
wished to telegraph for a nurse from London,
but Sir Edward had a horror of them, and
having recovered consciousness shook his
head vehemently when it was suggested; and
so it ended in Milly's nurse volunteering to
assist his valet in nursing him. Poor little

Milly wandered about the house with Fritz at her heels in a very woe-begone fashion. What with the anxiety in her heart lest her uncle should die, and the absence of her nurse–who could spare little time now to look after her–she felt most forlorn, and her greatest comfort was to go down to the keeper's cottage and talk to Mrs. Maxwell.

Sir Edward was soon out of danger, but he was a long time recovering, and required most careful nursing. Milly begged and entreated to go in and see him, but this was not allowed. At last permission was given by the doctor for a very short visit, and the child stole in on tiptoe, but insisted upon taking a large brown-paper parcel in with her, the contents of which were unknown to all except herself.

Softly she crept up to the bed, and looked at her uncle's bandaged head and worn face with the greatest awe.

He put out his hand, which she took in hers, and then she said, her brown eyes fixed wistfully on his face,—

'I've wanted to see you, Uncle Edward, for so long. I wish you would let me come in and help to nurse you.'

Sir Edward smiled, then shook his head.

'I've been asking God to make you better so many times,' she continued, softly stroking his hand as she spoke, 'and He is going to make you live again; now isn't He? I wasn't quite sure whether you mightn't like to die best, but I didn't want you to. Nurse says I mustn't stay a moment, but I've brought you a present. Maxwell went to the town and got it for me with the money Jack sent back to me. May I open it for you?'

Reading assent in his eyes, Milly eagerly removed her brown paper, and then lifted on to the bed with difficulty a picture of the Prodigal Son, in a plain oak frame.

'Isn't it a lovely one, Uncle Edward? There's the prodigal son—I've learned to say it properly now—all in rags hurrying along the road, and there's his old father in the distance coming to meet him; and can you see the words underneath?—then you can see it beautifully.'

Nurse came forward and helped the child to put the picture in the place she wished; and Sir Edward tried to look pleased, and said in a low tone,—

'Thank you, little one, I can see it well from there;' but under his breath he muttered, 'Has she a purpose in bringing that everlasting subject before me? I'm sick to death of it. I shall get rid of that picture when she is gone.'

But he did not. His eyes grew somewhat wistful as he gazed upon it, and later in the day, when nurse asked him if he would like to have it moved, he shook his head in the negative.

No one could know his thoughts during those long days and nights of weariness and pain; the restlessness of body did not equal the restlessness of soul, and the past came back with a startling vividness. The wasted years, the misused talents, and, above all, the fast-closed heart against its rightful Owner, now seemed to stand up in judgment against him. Often in his wretchedness would he groan aloud, and wish for unconsciousness to come to his aid and consign to oblivion his accusing memory.

It was a cold, grey afternoon. Mrs. Maxwell's little kitchen was in perfect order; the fire shed flickering lights on the bright dish-covers on the wall, and the blue and white china on the old-fashioned dresser was touched with a ruddy glow. Mrs. Maxwell herself, seated in a wooden rocking-chair, in spotless white apron, was knitting busily as she talked; and Milly on a low stool, the tabby in her arms, with her golden-brown curls in pretty disorder and her large, dark eyes gazing earnestly into the fire, completed the picture.

'Do you like winter, Mrs. Maxwell?' she was asking.

'Well, my dear, I can't say as I don't prefer the summer; but there!—the Almighty sends it, and it must be right, and I don't think folks have a right to grumble and go rushing off to them foreign parts, a-leaving their own country and the weather God gives them, because they say they must have sunshine. I allays thinks they've no sunshine in their hearts, or they wouldn't be so up and down with the weather.'

'I think winter is a very lonely time, Mrs. Maxwell, and I'm so sorry for the trees. I was out this morning with Fritz, and I talked to them and tried to cheer them up. And I think they feel they're nearly dead, poor things! And they were shivering with cold this morning; they were, really. I told them they would be happy when next summer comes, but they sighed and shook their heads; it's such a long time to wait, and they have nothing to do—they can only stand still. I was very sad this morning; after I had talked to them, I went down to the plantation at the bottom of the lawn, and on the way I came to a poor dead frog. Fritz sniffed at him, but he didn't seem to be sorry. I don't know how he died; I thought perhaps he had stayed out in the cold and got frozen, he felt so very cold. I took him up and buried him, and I wondered if his mother would miss him; and then I went on a little farther, and there were some little bird's feathers all in a heap on the ground. I felt sure a cruel cat had been eating it up, and

I couldn't help crying, for everything seemed to be dying. And when I got to the plantation I was a little comforted, for the fir-trees looked so comfortable and warm—they hadn't lost their leaves like the other trees—but do you know, in the middle of them all was a tall, thin, bare tree—he looked so lonely and unhappy, and he was the only one without any leaves.'

'One of those birches, I expect. My man, he said the other day that the fir plantation yonder wanted weeding out.'

'Well, I couldn't bear to see him so sad, so I crept right in amongst the firs until I got to him, and then I put my arms right round him and cuddled him tight. I told him God would take care of him, and give him a beautiful new green dress next summer; but he seemed to feel the cold, and I expect the other trees aren't very kind to him. I always think the firs are very stiff and proud. I—I kissed him before I came away; it was a sad morning.'

Milly's tones were truly pathetic, and Mrs. Maxwell, who loved to hear her childish fancies and never laughed at them, now looked up from her knitting sympathetically,–

'You're sad yourself, dear. Is your uncle pretty well to-day?'

'I think he is getting better, but he mustn't talk, and nurse won't let me see him. I think it's winter makes me sad, Mrs. Maxwell.'

There was silence for a few moments. Milly stroked her cat thoughtfully, then she said,—

'If uncle Edward had died, what would have happened to me? Should I have had to go to the workhouse?'

'Bless your little heart, no! Why, my man and I was saying the other day that it's most sure as you'll be mistress of the property one day. Sir Edward he have no other kith or kin as far as we know. Workhouse, indeed! A place where they takes in tramps and vagabonds.'

'I heard some of the maids talking about it,' pursued Milly; 'they said they wondered what would happen to me. I think he is my only uncle, so I couldn't go anywhere else. I wish I had a father, Mrs. Maxwell—I'm always wishing for one. I never remember my father.

My mother I do, but she was always ill, and she didn't like me to bother her. Do you know, I thought when I came to Uncle Edward that he would be a kind of father; Miss Kent said he would. But I'm afraid he doesn't like me to bother him either; I should like him to take me up in his arms and kiss me. Do you think he ever will? I feel as if no one cares for me sometimes.'

'I think a certain little apple dumpling as I put in the oven for some one is smelling as if it wants to come out,' was Mrs. Maxwell's brisk response as she bustled out of her chair, her old eyes moist with feeling.

In an instant Milly's pensiveness had disappeared. A baked apple dumpling had great charms for her, and no one would have believed that the light-hearted child with the merry laugh, now dancing round the room, and climbing up to the dresser for a plate, was the same as the one who had so sadly discoursed a few moments before on the mournfulness of winter and of her orphaned state.

'Did you make such nice apple dumplings for Tommy?' she asked presently, busy with her fork and spoon, and looking supremely content with herself and surroundings.

'Ah! Didn't I? I mind when he used to come in on Saturdays from the forge, I always had a hot pudding for him; he used to say there was no one who cooked as well as "mother." '

'He's a long time coming home, isn't he, Mrs. Maxwell? I get so tired of waiting. I wish he would come for Christmas.'

'I'm not tired of waiting,' Mrs. Maxwell said softly, 'and I've waited these nine years, but it sometimes seems as if it was only yesterday as he went off. I feel at times like fretting sadly over him, and wish I knew if he was alive or dead, but then the Lord do comfort one, and I know he sees just where he is, and He'll let me know when the right time comes.'

'I'm expecting him every day,' said Milly with a cheerful little nod. 'I was telling God about him last night at my window on the stairs—and it seemed as if God said to me that he was coming very soon now. I shouldn't wonder if he came next week!'

The keeper entered the cottage at this moment, and Milly jumped off her seat at once.

'I'm afraid it's time for me to be going back. Nurse said I was to be in at four. Are you going to take me, Mr. Maxwell?'

'Don't I always see you safe and sound up at the house?' Maxwell said good-humouredly, 'and do you know it has struck four ten minutes ago? When you and my Mrs. get together to have a crack, as the saying is, you don't know how time passes. We shall have to run for it.'

Milly was being rapidly covered up in a thick plaid by Mrs. Maxwell.

'There now, my dearie, good-bye till next I see you, and don't be doleful in that big house by yourself. Your uncle will soon be well, and nurse will be better able to see after you. I don't know what all those servants are after, that they can't amuse you a bit.'

'Nurse doesn't like me ever to go near the servants' hall,' said Milly; 'I promised her I wouldn't. Sarah stays in the nursery with me, but she runs away downstairs pretty often. Good-bye, Mrs. Maxwell.'

It was getting dark. Maxwell soon had the child in his strong arms, and was striding along at a great pace, when, passing a rather dark corner, a man suddenly sprang out of the bushes and took to his heels.

'Let me see you in here again, and it will be the worse for you, you scoundrel!'

'Oh, Maxwell,' cried Milly, 'who is it?'

'One of them skulking poachers—they're always in here after the rabbits. If I hadn't a-had you to look after, and had my thick stick, I would a-been after him.'

'But you wouldn't have hurt him?'

'I should have taught him a lesson, that I should!'

'But, Maxwell, you mustn't really! Only think, he might be—Tommy coming home! You couldn't see who it was, could you? It would be dreadful if you chased away Tommy.'

'No fear o' that,' Maxwell said in a quieter tone. 'My own son wouldn't skulk along like that. He was a ragged vagabond, that's what he was.'

'Prodigal sons are nearly always ragged; he might have been some one's prodigal son, Maxwell.'

'He was just a poacher, my dear, and I think I know the chap. He's staying at the Blue Dragon, and has been a-watching this place for some time.'

'Perhaps he is one of God's prodigal sons,' said Milly softly, 'like Jack was.'

To this Maxwell made no reply, but when he set her down in the brightly-lighted hall a little later, he said,—

'Don't you fret about our Tommy. I should know him fast enough. He wouldn't run from his own father.'

And Milly went in, and that night added another petition to her prayers:—

'And please, God, if the man who ran away from Maxwell is a prodigal son, bring him back to his father, for Jesus' sake. Amen.'

CHAPTER VII.

Cross-Examination.

NURSE, where is Miss Millicent? I haven't seen her for days. Fetch her in here this afternoon, and you go and get a little fresh air; I am well enough to be left alone now.'

Sir Edward's tone was impatient; he was getting to the convalescent stage, and nurse found him a most trying patient. Nothing would please him, and he wearied both himself and her with his perpetual complaints.

'I though she would only worry you, sir; she has been asking me every day to come in and see you. I will fetch her at once.'

Milly shortly appeared in a clean pinafore, her little face radiant with smiles. As she climbed up into the chair by the bedside and gently stroked the hand that was given her, she said with sparkling eyes,—

'Nurse says I may stay here all alone with you, uncle; won't that be lovely? May I give you your medicines, and be your nurse?'

'I can't promise that, but you may sit there and talk to me.'

'What shall I talk about?'

'Anything you like. You never seem to be at a loss for conversation.'

Milly considered for a moment.

'I've had so few people to talk to lately, you see; I generally talk most to Fritz. He understands, I'm sure, but he doesn't talk back. When will you be quite well again, uncle?'

'Not this side of Christmas, I'm afraid.'

'Oh, dear, what a long time! But I'm very glad God has made you better. Nurse said it was a mercy you hadn't broken your neck. Do you know, uncle, I saw such a sad sight yesterday morning. I was down in the fir plantation with Fritz, and we came upon a dear little rabbit caught in a steel trap. Maxwell said a poacher had put it there, and he was very angry. The rabbit was quite dead, and his two hind legs were broken. Wasn't it dreadful? What is a poacher, uncle?'

'A thief—a man who steals game that isn't his.'

'Maxwell says there are lots of poachers about. I'm so afraid he will think Tommy is one when he comes back. I do hope he will be careful, because if it's dark he might make a mistake. Wouldn't it be dreadful if he hurt his own prodigal son! And I expect Tommy will look very like a poacher. He is sure to have ragged, dirty clothes. If I was——'
Here Milly paused, and gazed dreamily in front of her for some minutes in silence.

'Well?' inquired Sir Edward, looking at his little niece with interest as she sat in the big chair, her elbows supported by her knees and her chin resting in her hands, 'are you going into a brown study?'

'I was just thinking if I was a prodigal son—
I mean a real one, not just playing at it, as I
do—I would rather be one of God's prodigal
sons, than belonging to any one else.'

'Why?'

'Because I would know for certain He would
meet me and take me back. Nurse told me
she had a cousin who ran away and made
himself a soldier, and when he was sorry and
wanted to come home, his father shut the
door in his face, and wouldn't let him in.
And then there's Tommy, I can't help
s'posing that his father mightn't know him.
But God can't make mistakes. It must be
lovely just to run right into God's arms, and
hear Him saying, "Bring forth the best robe,
and put it on him." I should love to have Him
say that to me.'

Milly's little face glowed with pleasure at
the thought, and she turned her expressive
eyes towards her uncle, who lay with knitted
brows listening to her.

'And supposing if God would not receive
you; supposing you had stayed away so long,
and had refused to listen to His voice when

He called, and then when you did want to come back, you felt it would be too late, what would you do then?'

Milly smiled.

'Why, uncle, it would never be too late for God, would it? Maxwell said he would be glad to see Tommy if he came back in the middle of the night, and God would never turn one of His prodigal sons away. He loves them so that He sent Jesus to die for them. He would never say He couldn't have them back again.'

Sir Edward said no more, and after another pause the child went on.

'I was asking Mrs. Maxwell the other day if she had some best clothes for Tommy when he came home, and she took me upstairs into his little room, and opened a long drawer, and told me to look inside. And there were his best Sunday coat and waistcoat and trousers, and a silk handkerchief with lavender in it, and a necktie with yellow and red stripes, and she told me they had been there for nine years, and she shakes them out and brushes them every Saturday. He didn't run away in his best clothes, you know; he left them behind. So they're quite ready for him. The only thing Mrs. Maxwell hasn't got is the ring.'

'The what?' inquired Sir Edward, amused.

'The ring,' Milly repeated earnestly. 'Maxwell will have to say, "Put a ring on his hand, and shoes on his feet." Mrs. Maxwell has got a pair of carpet slippers. I couldn't bear her not having shoes ready for him, so we looked about and found a pair that are just too small for Maxwell, and I put them in the drawer my own self. Mrs. Maxwell says he won't want a ring, and that she thinks the Bible people dressed differently, and she said Tommy was a poor man's son: it wasn't as if he was rich. But I don't know; I don't like to think we have no ring for him. I suppose you haven't one, uncle, that you would like to give him?'

Sir Edward put his head back on his cushions and laughed aloud. Then, noting Milly's troubled face, he said,—

'Wait till Tommy comes back, little woman, and then it will be time enough to see about his ring, though I quite agree with his mother that it would be most unfitting.'

'You have had the picture I gave you taken away, uncle,' said Milly presently, her quick eyes roving around the room. 'Ah! you've had it hung up on the wall. That's nice there. You can see it from your bed. Don't you like looking at it? Doesn't it make you feel happy?'

'I can't say it does,' replied Sir Edward, glancing at the picture in question. 'Why ought it to make me feel happy?'

'Oh, it's so nice to think he is just getting home after being away so long. I wonder if he was a great time walking back. How long do you think it takes one of God's prodigal sons to get back to Him, uncle?'

'I should say a very long time indeed,' said Sir Edward slowly.

'But how long? Two days, or six hours, or a week?'

'It would depend perhaps on how long they had been away from Him.'

'It's rather hard to understand,' said Milly, wrinkling her little brow perplexedly, 'because God is everywhere, isn't He? and I should have thought He would have been close by them all the time. I was asking nurse about it, and she said that God was near them, only they wouldn't have anything to say to Him, and did bad things and shut the Lord Jesus out of their heart, and let Satan in, and then God had to leave them till they said they were sorry. I suppose directly they say, "Father, I have sinned against Heaven and in Thy sight, and am no more worthy to be called Thy son," then God just folds them in His arms and forgives them and takes them back again; isn't that it?'

'Look here, I think we have had enough of this subject. Talk about something else.'

Sir Edward's tone was irritable; Milly's ready tongue obeyed.

'Nurse says it's so cold to-day that she thinks it will snow. Do you think it will? It is quite smoky by the river; nurse says it is a fog. I wondered where it all came from. Do you think it might be God's breath, uncle?'

As she was chatting on, suddenly there came a sharp knock at the door, and a visitor appeared.

'Thought I'd look you up, for I heard you were on the sick list. Good gracious! you have been pretty bad, haven't you? Will you put me up for a night or two? I expect you want a little cheerful company.'

Talking volubly, Major Lovell—for it was he—came forward and looked with real concern on Sir Edward's altered face.

'I'm very glad to see you,' said the latter heartily, holding out his hand. 'Come and stay for as long as you like. I'm sick to death of my own society.'

'And is this the small party that arrived so unexpectedly when I was here before?' inquired Major Lovell, looking down at Milly, who still sat in the big chair regarding the newcomer with her large brown eyes.

'Yes,' said Sir Edward, a faint smile hovering about his lips as he remembered his horror of her advent; 'she is taking charge of me this afternoon.'

Milly held out her little hand with all the grace of a duchess.

'I remember you,' she said; 'you were one of the gentlemen that laughed at me.'

'I don't think I could have been guilty of such rudeness, surely.'

'Now I think you may run away,' Sir Edward said; 'and tell nurse I will ring when I want her.'

Milly obeyed, and confided to nurse that she hoped the 'new gentleman' would not keep her away from her uncle. 'For do you know, nurse, I like Uncle Edward so much better when he is in bed. He looks so sad, and speaks so softly. I wish I could sit with him every day.'

Major Lovell was a distant cousin of Sir Edward, and there existed a warm friendship between them. The very brightness of his tone seemed to do the invalid good, and Milly was quite delighted to find that her uncle's visitor not only listened with interest to the account of her favourite games and pastimes, but insisted upon joining her in them, and the walls of the quiet old house rang again with merry mirth and laughter such as they had not known for years.

Upstairs in the sick-room Major Lovell proved a wonderfully patient and skilful nurse; but there were times when all his bright cheeriness could not smooth the furrows in the invalid's brow, or take away the fretfulness of tone.

One morning Major Lovell came down from an interview with him with a puzzled expression of face. Catching sight of Milly in the hall, equipped in hat and jacket, he asked,—

'Are you going out with nurse?'

'No, nurse is busy—just by my own self, in the avenue with Fritz. Do come with me.'

The major consented, but with a graver face than usual; and then suddenly, very full of his own thoughts, said to the child,—

'I believe your uncle has something on his mind. It strikes me from different things he has let drop that he is turning pious.'

'What is pious?'[2] inquired Milly instantly.

---

[2] *pious* – Godly; reverencing and honoring the

'What is it? A pious person thinks every one wicked but themselves, and condemns everybody and everything all round them. They are most objectionable people, little woman, so mind you never take up that line; and the worst of it is that they're so satisfied with their own goodness, that you can't crush them, try as much as you may.'

'And is Uncle Edward going to be like them?' asked the child, with a perplexed face.

'I devoutly hope not. I shall do all in my power to prevent it.'

'What do pious people do?' questioned Milly.

'Do! They give tracts away and sing hymns, and pull long faces over very well-bound Bibles.'

'I like singing hymns,' asserted Milly very emphatically; 'everybody sings hymns to God, don't they? I listen to the birds,

---

Supreme Being in heart and in the practice of the duties he has enjoined; having due veneration and affection for the character of God, and habitually obeying his commands. (From Noah Webster's 1828 American Dictionary of the English Language.)

sometimes, and wish I could sing like them; and the trees sing, and the bees and flies. Everything seems to sing out of doors in the summer time, but they've nearly all dropped asleep now till next year. What hymns do you sing, Major Lovell?'

'Bless the child! what do you take me for?' and the major laughed heartily as he spoke; then, with a twinkle in his eye, he went on gravely, 'I shall begin to think that you are pious, if you don't take care. What else do you do besides sing hymns?'

'I have a Bible,' said Milly solemnly, 'and I just love it.'

'And what makes you love such a dry book as the Bible? You can't understand a word of it.'

'Oh, I can, Major Lovell; it's beautiful. I love nurse to read and read it to me. It tells about Jesus, you know, and I love Jesus, and he loves me. And it has such nice stories in it.'

Major Lovell gave a long, low whistle.

'Ah!' he said, shaking his head comically at the little figure walking by his side, 'I'm very

much afraid you may be at the bottom of it
all. Do you read the Bible to your uncle? Do
you tell him that he has been wasting his life
and not fulfilling the end for which he was
created; in fact, that he is a wicked sinner?
For that has been the substance of his talk
with me this morning!'

'Uncle Edward is a very good man,' Milly
replied warmly. 'I don't know what you
mean, Major Lovell; don't you read the
Bible?'

'What will you think of me if I tell you I
don't?'

'Perhaps you know it all by heart? I expect
that is why.'

'I rather think I don't. You must not begin
to catechise me too severely. Who has
brought you up in this pious fashion?'

'I'm not pious—you said they were horrid
people—but I thought all the grown-up
people read the Bible, except people like
Jack.'

'Who is Jack?'

'He was a prodigal son, one of God's
prodigal sons.'

'And what are they, may I ask?'

Milly did not answer for a minute, then she stopped short, and said very solemnly, raising her large dark eyes to the major's face,—

'I wonder if you're a prodigal son? Uncle Edward said there were some rich ones. Have you run away from God, Major Lovell?'

'Oh, come now,' said the major, pinching her cheek good-naturedly; 'I didn't bargain for this when I came out with you. You must keep your sermons for some one else. Come along to the stables with me, and I will give you a ride.'

In an instant Milly's gravity disappeared, and a little time afterwards she was laughing gleefully as she was being trotted round the stable-yard on a large bay mare; but she said to her nurse when she came in,—

'Major Lovell is very nice, but very funny, and I can't always understand his talk; he says such difficult things.'

CHAPTER VIII.

'He Arose and Came to His Father.'

MAJOR LOVELL stayed a week, and Sir Edward seemed the better for his company, as far as his bodily health was concerned. But at heart he was very wretched, and his cousin's influence was not the sort to help him.

'Now, old chap, make haste and get well, and don't moon over yourself and your feelings. And come down to our place for Christmas, won't you? You're getting quite in the blues by being so much alone.'

These were Major Lovell's parting words, and Sir Edward responded, 'No, thanks: I prefer being at home this Christmas. Why, I doubt if I shall leave my room by that time; I am as weak as a baby.'

The week before Christmas Sir Edward was in an easy-chair in the library, and, though still an invalid, was now making rapid progress towards recovery. He was conning over an article he had just written, before a blazing fire, when there was a knock at the door. A frown came to his face as he turned to see who the intruder was, but disappeared at the sight of his little niece, rosy and breathless, in out-door garments, and hugging a large piece of holly in her arms.

'Uncle Edward, he has come!'

'Who has come?'

'Tommy—he really and truly has. Ford told me just as I came in with nurse. He heard it from Harris, and Harris heard it from Maxwell himself. He said, "My lad has come, tell little missy," and Ford says Harris said, "He looked as if he could dance a jig for joy!" Oh, Uncle Edward, may I go to them? Nurse says it's too late, but I do want to be there. There's such a lot to be done now he has really come; and Uncle Edward, may they kill one of the cows in the farm that are being fatted up? There's no calf, I'm afraid. May they? And may I go and tell them so? You will let me go, won't you?'

'Most certainly not; it is much too late in the afternoon for you to be going down there—it is getting quite dark; and as to one of my cattle being disposed of in that way, I should not dream of allowing it for one moment.'

Milly's eyes filled with tears, which she vainly tried to restrain: when her uncle spoke to her in that tone she knew it was useless to remonstrate.

'They'll be having the feast without me,' she said, with a little sob in her voice. 'Mrs. Maxwell promised me I should be there when they had it, and I'm longing to see Tommy.'

'Then if Mrs. Maxwell promised you that, she will put off her feast till to-morrow,' said Sir Edward in a softer tone. 'And now be a sensible little woman, and wait patiently till the time comes. You may be sure his parents will like to have him to themselves the first night. Run away now; I don't want to be disturbed.'

Poor little Milly crept out of the room feeling very crestfallen, and a short time after was lying on the hearthrug before the nursery fire, her arms wound round Fritz's neck, confiding to him the whole story, and comforting herself by conjecturing how and where the meeting had taken place. Her little mind was so full of the subject that it was long before nurse could get her to sleep that night. He last words before she dropped off were,—

'I wonder who will do the music and dancing!'

The next morning, the instant her breakfast was over, Milly obtained nurse's permission to go down to the keeper's cottage under charge of Sarah, the nursery-maid. She was away the whole morning, and about one o'clock a message came from Mrs. Maxwell to ask if she might stay to dinner with them. So that it was not till nearly four in the afternoon that she was brought up to the house, and then, flushed and excited, she poured into her nurse's ear a long account of all that she had been hearing and doing.

'Now come, my dear, you mustn't talk for ever,' was nurse's remonstrance at last; 'Sir Edward told me I could send you to him for a little when you came in, and I must make you tidy first.'

It was quite dusk when Milly entered the library, but the bright firelight showed her the figure of her uncle leaning back in his easy-chair, and indulging in a reverie.

'Well,' he said, looking round, 'where have you been all day? Down at Maxwell's, I suppose?'

'Yes,' said Milly sedately, 'and I'll tell you all about it if you like. May I make myself comfortable first?'

And after a minute's hesitation she climbed into the heavy armchair on the opposite side of the fireplace, making a pretty picture, as she leant her curly head back on the cushion and gazed earnestly into her uncle's face.

'We will have a crack together, uncle. That's what Maxwell calls it, when Mrs. Maxwell and I talk over the fire. May I tell you all about Tommy now?'

'You may,' was the amused reply.

'Well, you know, I ran as fast as I could down to the wood this morning, and Sarah ran after me, and Mrs. Maxwell saw me coming, and she ran to the door. I was rather out of breath, you see, so she just smoothed me down a little, and we kissed each other, and she cried a tiny bit, for I felt her tears on my face. Then she took me in to see Tommy—Maxwell was out, and Tommy was in the kitchen in one of Maxwell's greatcoats, and he was eating some bacon at the table for his breakfast. He got up when he saw me— he's a nice big man, uncle, but I think his hair wants cutting. We shook hands, and I told him I'd been expecting him ever so long; he looked rather shy, but after he had quite finished his breakfast, we had a very nice talk, and Mrs. Maxwell went bustling about getting dinner ready. Tommy told me all about himself from the very beginning, but I really quite forget some of it. He never kept any pigs at all, but he kept some sheep instead—he went out to America and did it— and then he was a railway man, and then he had a fever, and then he got into bad company, and at last he came to London, and he was an omnibus man there, and then a cabman, and then he drank too much beer, and his money all went away, and he was ashamed of himself, and so he wouldn't write home, and then he smashed his cab against a lamp-post, and then he drank too much again.'

'I don't think you need tell me any more of his misdoings,' said Sir Edward drily.

'But, you see, he had to get very bad before he got good, because he was a prodigal son. And he is sorry now. He said he never, never would have come home until he was a good man, only one day he listened to a man preaching a sermon in the middle of a street on a Sunday night, and he felt uncomfortable, and then he was spoken to after by—— Now guess, uncle, who do you think?'

Sir Edward could not guess, so Milly went on triumphantly: 'Why, it was my Jack, and he began to talk to him, and told him he was like him once, and he said he was looking out for a Tommy Maxwell. Now wasn't that wonderful, when it was Tommy himself he spoke to! Well, Tommy said he hadn't the face to go home till he was better, but Jack told him not to wait a day longer, for his father and mother were waiting for him; but the strange thing was that even then Tommy waited a whole two weeks before he made up his mind to come. Now don't you think he was foolish, uncle?'

'Very foolish.'

'I couldn't quite understand it, but nurse say there are lots of people like that, waiting to make themselves better, instead of running home just as they are. She says some of God's prodigal sons do that; do you think many do, uncle?'

'I daresay.'

'And Tommy said, though he wanted to see his home again dreadfully, he had a great fight with himself to come at all. I didn't know prodigal sons found it so difficult—the one in the Bible didn't, not when he once made up his mind. Well, and so Tommy got out at the station—I'm sorry he came by train, but Jack's uncle paid for his ticket—I would rather he had run the whole way.'

'Why would you?' asked Sir Edward with a smile.

'I think it would have been more proper if he had,' said the child slowly, her head a little on one side, as she gazed thoughtfully into the fire. 'I always run or walk the whole way when I play the prodigal son. I begin rather slowly, because it looks a long way off, but when I come near I hurry. I'm wanting to be there when I see my home. The prodigal son didn't have a train in the Bible, and I think Tommy might have tried to do without it!'

The tone of reproach at the end of her speech was too much for her uncle's gravity, and he laughed aloud. 'I am afraid Tommy has sadly disappointed you. Did he take a cab from the station?'

'No, he didn't do that. He got home in the afternoon, and Maxwell was cleaning his gun on the doorstep when he saw a shadow, and he looked up, and there he was. Oh! I should like to have been there; but I'm sorry to say Maxwell didn't fall on his neck and kiss him. I asked Tommy very carefully about it, and he said he took hold of both of his hands and squeezed them tight, and he gave a shout; and Mrs. Maxwell was doing her washing in the back yard, and she heard it, and she shook all over so that she could hardly walk. She cried so much when she saw Tommy that Maxwell had to pat her on the back and give her a glass of water; and Tommy, he sat down on the little seat inside the porch, and he said—these were his very words, uncle—"I ain't fit to come home, father. I'm a disgrace to your name," and Mrs. Maxwell—Tommy told me—she just took his head between her two hands and drew it to rest on her shoulder, and then she bent down and kissed him all over, and she said: "My boy, who should you come to when you are in disgrace and trouble but your own father and mother?"'

'Tommy said, when he told me this, "It fair broke my heart, miss," and then he gave a great sob, and I began to cry, and then Mrs. Maxwell came up, and her hands were all floury, for she was making an apple pudding, and she cried too, and then we all cried together—at least, Tommy turned his head away, and pretended he didn't, but I saw he did.'

Milly paused for breath, and her eyes looked wistfully into the glowing coals before her.

'I didn't know prodigal sons were sad when they came back, but Tommy seemed so sad that he made me sad, too. Why do you think Tommy cried, uncle?'

Sir Edward did not reply; he was gazing dreamily into the fire, and something of the wistfulness in his little niece's face seemed to be reflected in his. He gave a start after a moment's silence.

'Eh, child? What are you saying? Have you finished your story?'

'Why, no, uncle, not nearly. Are you tired? Nurse said I must not tire you too much.'

Sir Edward laughed, but it was not a happy laugh.

'Oh, finish your story by all means, little woman,' he said; and Milly continued:—

'We all cheered up when Mrs. Maxwell asked me if I'd like to stay to dinner. I asked if it was the feast, and she laughed and said "Yes." She had a roast leg of pork in the oven, with some stuffing and apple sauce, and uncle, it was lovely! Maxwell came in just in time, and he looked so happy, and then we all sat down to dinner; but I asked Maxwell to say first, before we began: "Let us eat, and be merry, for this my son was dead, and is alive again, he was lost, and is found." He folded his hands and said it like grace, and Mrs. Maxwell said "Amen" when he had finished, and wiped her eyes with her apron. I told them we must all be very merry, but Tommy wasn't, I'm afraid. He kept looking first at Mrs. Maxwell and then all round the kitchen, and then at Maxwell, and the he sighed very big sighs. He said he couldn't believe he was at home, but he told me, when I asked him quietly afterwards, that he was really very happy, he only sighed and looked sad because he thought how foolish he had been to stay away so long. I was very sorry for one thing about him, uncle. He wasn't in his best clothes, they were all too small for him, and the slippers wouldn't fit him, but Maxwell says he will buy him some new ones to-morrow. And Tommy told me he wouldn't wear a ring if he had one. He asked me why he should, so I told him about the prodigal son in the Bible—he seemed to like hearing about it, and he said he thought he was very like him. And then I asked about the music and dancing. I wanted to have that, but we couldn't manage it. Mrs. Maxwell said we had music in our hearts; how can we have that, uncle? I didn't hear any in mine, for I kept quite silent and listened for it.'

'I expect she meant you were so happy that you did not want any music to make you happier.'

'I was very happy. Oh, Uncle Edward, why don't all the prodigal sons go home? I can't think why they like staying away. It is so lovely to think of Tommy now! And every one would be just as happy, wouldn't they?'

'I don't think all young men have such fond parents as your friend Tommy has,' said Sir Edward gravely.

'Haven't they? Well, God's prodigal sons couldn't have a nicer Father. I lie and think of them when I'm in bed sometimes, and I talk to God about them. I was so glad when Jack went back to Him. I think it is worst of all to stay a long way off from God, because he does love them so. I wonder if it is that they don't know whether God will take them back. Tommy seemed half afraid, till he came, that his father would be angry with him. I should like to see a prodigal son running back into God's arms so much! But I suppose he does it very quietly, and only the angels look down and see it!'

'And what is this young scapegrace going to do now? Live on his father and mother, or is he going to try and do some honest work?'

Sir Edward's tone was rather impatient. Milly looked up, surprised.

'Do you mean Tommy, uncle? Are you angry with him? He told me he was going to look for work directly, and Maxwell is coming up to speak to you about him to-morrow.'

'Ah! I daresay—wants him to take the place of under-keeper, I suppose, and Sir Edward gave a little grunt of dissatisfaction at the thought.

CHAPTER IX.

'A Little Child Shall Lead Them.'

WHEN Sir Edward retired to his room that night, he paced up and down for some time in front of the picture that his little niece had given him. His brow was knitted, and he was thinking deeply.

'I am longing to have peace,' he muttered. "why cannot I make up my mind to seek it! "I will arise"—ay, easy to say—it's a hard and bitter thing for a backslider to retrace his steps. How the child stabs me sometimes, and how little she knows my past!'

He stopped and gazed at the picture. 'And the Lord Himself used this as an illustration. I could not want anything stronger.'

A deep-drawn sigh followed, then a heartfelt cry rose to heaven.

'May God have mercy on me, and bring me back, for I can't bring myself!'

The next morning Sir Edward had an interview with his keeper, who brought his son up with him; and as the tall, broad-shouldered young fellow stood before the squire, and in earnest, humble tones asked if he could be given a chance of redeeming his character by being employed on the estate, Sir Edward's severity relaxed, and after a long conversation with him he promised he would give him a trial.

He smiled grimly to himself as father and son left him with warm expressions of gratitude.

'So that is the child's hero! One whose example I might well follow. He has had the courage at last to take the step from which I am still shrinking. Why should I fear that my welcome home would be less full of love and forgiveness than his?'

It was Christmas Eve: a wild and stormy day; the wind raged ceaselessly round the old house, howling down the chimneys, and beating the branches of the trees outside against the window panes.

Milly had been very busy for some hours helping Ford to decorate the hall and rooms with holly and evergreen, though Ford would every now and then pause in his work, saying, 'There, Miss Milly, I'm sure we're overdoing it; if the house was full of company now, I would take a pride in it, but I don't believe the master will notice whether it's done or not. It seems to me as he is getting more and more shut up into hisself lately. Christmas is a dull time with us.'

All was finished at last, and Milly went up to the nursery and stood at the window, her bright brown eyes eagerly scanning and taking note of every object out of doors.

'It's a perfect hurricane,' said nurse presently, as she sat with her work in a comfortable chair by the fire. 'If we feel it inland like this, what must it be at sea!'

'I should like to be on the sea,' said Milly. 'I love the winds, but I think it is getting a little bit too rough this afternoon. I'm rather afraid it will hurt the little trees. Ford said if I went out I should be blown away. Do you think, nurse, if the wind was very, very strong, it would ever be able to blow me up to heaven?'

'I am afraid not,' said nurse gravely, 'and I don't think we could spare you, my dear. You would not like to leave this world yet awhile.'

'Sometimes I think I should, and sometimes I think I shouldn't. I think I should like to be blown up to spend a day there, and then come back again. Oh, nurse, Goliath is screaming and cracking so; I wish the wind would knock him over—he is a horrid old tree. I always think he is making faces at me when I run past him. Wouldn't it be nice to see him blown down?'

'You mustn't wish that,' said nurse, getting up from her chair and moving towards the door; 'it's a dangerous thing for an old tree to be blown down. Now I am going downstairs for a short time, so be a good child and don't get into mischief while I am away.'

Milly remained at the window for some minutes after nurse's departure, then her quick eyes noticed a poor wretched little kitten mewing pitifully as she vainly tried to shelter herself from the violent blasts around by crusting close to a tree.

In an instant, without thought of consequences, the child darted to the nursery door and down the broad oak staircase.

'Poor pussy! I will run and fetch her in. I expect she has run away from the kitchen.'

Sir Edward was writing at his study-table, when an unusually violent gust of wind caused him to raise his eyes and glance out of the window. There, to his amazement, he saw, under the old oak-tree on the lawn, his little niece, her golden brown curls flying as she battled with the elements, and struggled vainly to stoop and take the kitten in her arms.

He started up from his seat, but as he did so a blast that shook the house swept by; there was an awful cracking, then a crash, and, to his horror, a huge limb of the old oak came with an awful thud upon the very spot where his little niece was standing.

'My God, save her!' was his agonized cry, as he saw at the same moment the little figure stagger and fall. Then, forgetting his weakness and lack of physical strength, he dashed out of the house, and in another instant was standing over her.

His first feeling was one of intense thankfulness to find that the branch in falling could have only slightly grazed her, as she was lying on the ground untouched by it; but as he raised the motionless figure, and noted a red mark on her forehead which was swelling rapidly, his heart sank within him. It did not take him long to carry her into the house, and he was met at the door by nurse, who wisely wasted no time in useless lamentation, but set to work at once to restore animation to her little charge. Her efforts were successful. Milly was only slightly stunned, but it had been a miraculous escape, and had the blow been an inch nearer her temple it might have been fatal.   As it was, the child was more frightened than hurt, and when a little time after her uncle took her in his arms with unwonted tenderness, she clung to him and burst into passionate sobs.

'Take care of me, uncle!   That nasty old Goliath!   He tried to kill me, he did!   I saw him coming on the top of me.   God only just saved me in time, didn't He?'

When the bruise had been bathed and dressed by nurse, Sir Edward still kept her on his knee, and after nurse had left the room, and the child rested her little head on his shoulder in a very subdued frame of mind, he did, what he had never done yet—stooped over her and kissed her, saying:

'You have been very near death this afternoon, little one, and I could ill have spared you.'

Milly raised her large dark eyes to his.

'If I had died I should have gone straight up to God, shouldn't I?'

'Yes, you would.'

'I should have liked that. I suppose He doesn't want me yet, or He would have sent for me.'

When she came down to her uncle that evening she raised a very sad little face to his from the opposite side of the table.

'Uncle Edward, have you heard who Goliath really did kill?'

'Do you mean the tree that came on you? No one else was hurt, I hope?' and Sir Edward's tone was a little anxious.

'She was killed dead—quite dead and mangled, nurse said. It was the poor little kitten, uncle, that I ran out to fetch.'

The brown eyes were swimming with tears, and Milly could not understand the smile that came to Sir Edward's lips.

'Only a kitten! Well, it was sad, I daresay, but there are plenty of kittens about the place.'

'But, uncle, I've been thinking so much about this one. Ford says she had run away from the stable. I expect she was going to be a prodigal kitten, perhaps, and now she'll never run away any more. It's so sad about

her, and I think why it is sad is because
nobody cares, not even nurse. She said she
would rather it had been the kitten than me.
Poor little kitty, her mother will be missing
her so to-night! Do you think, uncle, the
wind or Goliath killed her? I think it was
Goliath. I just looked out of my window on
the stairs before I came down. The wind has
stopped now, and the trees seemed to be
crying and sobbing together. I'm sure they
were sorry for kitty. I think they were tired
out themselves, too, they have been so
knocked about to-day. I wish so much I had
been just in time to save the dear little kitten.'

'We will not talk about her any more,' said
Sir Edward cheerfully. 'Have you seem Tom
Maxwell lately?'

Milly's little tongue was only too ready to
talk of him. 'He helped nurse and me to get
some holly in the wood yesterday. I have nice
talks with him often. He says he is very
happy, and this will be the best Christmas he
has spent in his life. Uncle, I want to ask you
something. I've been thinking of it a great
deal to-day, only since I was knocked down

this afternoon I've had such a pain in my head I left off thinking. But I've just remembered it now. You see, it is really Jesus Christ's birthday to-morrow, and I was thinking I've been getting presents for every one in the house but Him. Nurse has been helping me with some of them. I've made nurse a kettleholder, and cook a needlebook, and I've bought a penknife for Ford, and a thimble for Sarah, and some handkerchiefs for Maxwell and Mrs. Maxwell, and some woollen gloves for Tommy. And I've nothing—no, nothing for Him. If I only knew something He would like.'

She paused, and a soft wistfulness came into her eyes. 'I was thinking,' she went on, 'that perhaps I could put my present for Him outside the nursery window on the ledge. And then when we are all in bed, and it is very quiet, I expect He might send an angel down to bring it up to Him. I think He might do that, because he knows how much I want to give Him something. But then I don't know what to give Him. Could you tell me, uncle?'

'I think,' said Sir Edward gravely, 'the only way you can give Him a Christmas present is to give something to the poor. He would rather have that. I will give you this to put in the plate to-morrow in church.'

And Sir Edward put his hand in his pocket, and rolled a sovereign across the table to his little niece.

But Milly was not satisfied.

'This is your present,' she said doubtfully. 'What will you give Him this Christmas besides? Is money the only thing you can give Him, uncle?'

Sir Edward pushed back his chair and rose from the table. His feelings were almost getting beyond his control. With the one subject that was now always foremost in his thoughts, the child's question rang again in his ears, 'Is money the only thing you can give Him, uncle?' And like a flash of light came a reply:

'No, I can give myself back to Him, my soul and body, that have now been so long in the keeping of His enemy.'

After a few minutes' silence, he said, in a strangely quiet voice,—

'Come, little one, it is bedtime; say "Good-night," and run up to nurse!'

Milly came up to him, and as he stood with his back to the fire warming his hands, she took hold of the ends of his coat in her little hands, and, looking up at him, said,—

'Uncle Edward, you gave me a kiss like a father might have done this afternoon. Would you mind very much giving me another?'

Sir Edward looked down at the sweet little face raised so coaxingly to his, and then took her up in his arms; but after he had given her the desired kiss he said, with some effort,—

'I want you to do something to-night, little one. When you say your prayers, ask that one of God's prodigal sons may be brought back this Christmas-time. It is one who wants to return. Will you pray for him?'

'Yes, uncle,' replied the child softly. 'And will you tell me his name?'

Something in his face made his little niece refrain from asking further questions. She left him a moment later, and Sir Edward went to the study and seated himself in a chair by the fire. The chimes of the village church were ringing out merrily, and presently outside in the avenue a little company of carol singers were singing the sweet old Christmas truths that none can hear untouched.

'Glory to God in the highest, and on earth peace, good will toward men.'

A sense of the love of God seemed to surround his soul, and this verse came into his mind as he mused:

'I have loved thee with an everlasting love, therefore with loving-kindness have I drawn thee.'

Could he not trace in the events of the last few months the hand of a loving Father gently calling His wanderer home? Stricken down himself, placed on a sick-bed for reflection, brought to the edge of the valley of the shadow of death, and then tenderly restored to life and health; the gentle voice and life of a little child pleading with him day by day, and that life having so lately been miraculously preserved from a great danger,—all this filled his heart wit the realisation of the mercy and loving-kindness of God; and when again the past came up before him, and the tempter drew near again with the old refrain, 'You have wandered too long, you have hardened your heart, and God has shut His ear to your cry,' Sir Edward, by the help and power of the Divine Spirit, was able to look up, and say from the depths of his heart,—

'Father, I have sinned against heaven, and in Thy sight, and am no more worthy to be called Thy son.'

They were sitting in the study the next afternoon, the child upon his knee, when Sir Edward said suddenly,—

'Do you know that I have received a letter to-day about you?'

'Who from?' asked Milly, with interest.

'From my sister, your aunt, in Australia. I wrote to her when you came, and she wants to have you out there, and bring you up amongst her own children. She says a friend of hers will take charge of you and take you to her next month. I must talk to nurse about it.'

The little hands clutched hold of his coat sleeve tightly, but not a word did Milly say.

Sir Edward noted a slight quivering of the lips, and a piteous gleam in the soft brown eyes. He waited in silence for a moment, then said cheerfully,—

'Won't you be glad to have a lot of boys and girls to play with, instead of staying here with a lonely old man?'

Still the child said nothing; but suddenly down went the curly head upon his arm, and the tears came thick and fast.

Sir Edward raised the little face to his.

'We must not have tears on Christmas Day,' he said. 'What is the matter? don't you want to go?'

'I suppose I must,' sobbed Milly. 'Ford told nurse the day I came that you hated children. I've always been thinking of it, but you have been so kind to me that I thought perhaps he had made a little mistake. Miss Kent didn't want me, and now you don't want me, and perhaps my aunt won't want me when I get there. I wish God wanted me, but I'm afraid He doesn't. Nurse says she thinks He wants me to work for Him when I grow up. I think—I think I'm rather like the little kitten yesterday, that nobody was sorry for when she died. You said there were plenty more kittens, didn't you?'

'I don't think there are plenty of small Millicents in this world,' and Sir Edward's voice was husky. 'Now listen, little woman; I have been thinking over the matter, and have decided this afternoon to keep you with me. I find I do want you after all, and cannot afford to lose you. Supposing we dry these tears, and talk about something else.'

And as the little arms were thrown round his neck, and a face full of smiles and tears like an April shower was lifted to his, the 'confirmed old bachelor' took to his heart the little maiden whose very existence had so annoyed and distressed him only a few months before.

'Uncle Edward,' she said, a little time after, 'do you know if that prodigal son you told me about last night has come back to God?'

Sir Edward was silent for a minute, then very gravely and solemnly he said:

'I think he has, little one. It has been a very happy Christmas Day to him, and you must pray now that he may not be ashamed to own his Lord, who has so mercifully brought him back through the instrumentality, innocence and love of one of His lambs.'

FINIS.

Tom Gillies MRS. GEORGE GLADSTONE

Tom Gillies and Dick Potter secretly meet at their favorite cave to concoct their plans for the day and plot the mischievous schemes which have given them so bad a name on Norton Island. The townspeople complain that the island is too small to hold such troublesome boys. Tom is sent away to work, where he learns that his bad habits have fastened strong chains around him, and sin has tied binding knots, making him a prisoner. He discovers the One who can untie those dreadful knots and free him to live a productive life among the people of Norton Island.

The Children of Cloverley HESBA STRETTON

Every day, in all the little common things as well as the great ones, we are to do the will of God. But when we love the level of comfort we have attained and the plans we have for the future, it is hard to say, "Thy will be done." The children of Cloverley not only say it—they do it. This dramatic adventure gives hope and courage, and will touch the heart of each family member.

Fire in the Sky (formerly *The Stolen Child*) CHRISTOPH VON SCHMID

An incredible story and "new favorite!" Little Henry is taken hostage by a band of robbers and lives for years in a dark cave. When he stumbles upon a crevice in the wall, he experiences with wonder the brilliance of the sun and the magnificence of the vast blue sky. He learns about the miracle of a tiny seed and the expression of love it represents. This creative work will give you a fresh appreciation for the natural wonders of creation that we so often take for granted.

That Printer of Udell's HAROLD BELL WRIGHT

President Ronald Reagon wrote: "That book, *That Printer of Udell's*, had an impact I shall always remember… The term "role model" was not a familiar term in that time and place. But I realize I found a role model in that traveling printer whom Harold Bell Wright had brought to life. He set me on a course I've tried to follow even unto this day. I shall always be grateful." (Written March 13, 1984, to Jean Wright, the second wife of Norman Wright, Harold Bell Wright's youngest son.)

A Puzzling Pair AMY LEFEUVRE

Inseparable twins, Guy and Berry are bursting with creativity and spunk. They are on a mission…to fill Guy's very big picture of the second coming of Jesus with all the people who are ready to meet Him! But his picture must be true, and time is running out! This rather unique approach to evangelism is as pure, bold, and simple as it gets!

Probable Sons AMY LEFEUVRE

Probable Sons etches into our hearts the importance of forgiveness and reconciliation. The delightful story will keep you smiling as our little heroine Milly boldly and innocently exhorts "probable (prodigal) sons" to return home. May the truths found in this little story find a resting place in the many hearts that have strayed far from home.

The Stranger At Home VARIOUS AUTHORS

The Stranger at Home, along with its accompanying stories, might seem a little "hard-edged," but it aptly challenges us to reconsider our God-given roles as parents and children. The folly of permissive parenting, and the inevitable consequences of obstinacy, disobedience, lying, and vanity are brought forth with "not-so-subtle" clarity, yet permeated with life-changing truths.

Winter's Folly MRS. O. F. WALTON

This is the tender story of lonely Old Man Winter, who demonstrates the epitome of selfless love. But all is not lost as young Myrtle, through her childlike innocence, rekindles his desire to live. This true-to-life story reminds us once again that when life seems to hold more than we can bear, we can rest assured that we have a loving God who is orchestrating events for our good.

Fireside Readings Vol. I and II VARIOUS AUTHORS

Lamplighter's collection of fireside readings gently instills virtuous qualities such as honesty, integrity, loyalty, courage and perseverance into the very fabric of our lives. Through unforgettable events, common, everyday boys and girls become heroes as they overcome temptation and courageously fight the adversary. Our children will want to be more like them—in fact, they will long to be.

Enoch Roden's Training HESBA STRETTON

This book is bursting with life's lessons! Through severe trials, Enoch learns much about sound business principles, sacrifice, and trusting God. If he had only said, "I am working with God…" he would never have found his work wearisome, for of all grand, and comforting, and heart-refreshing thoughts in this world, the greatest is the thought that we are co-workers with God. Without a doubt, after reading this book, you'll walk away a better person than when you began.

Ishmael MRS. E.D.E.N. SOUTHWORTH

Ishmael is founded on the life of one of the noblest of our countrymen who really lived, suffered, toiled, and triumphed in this land. Its inspirations of wisdom and goodness were drawn from the examples of heroic warriors and statesmen of the Revolution. Ishmael—born in the depths of poverty, misery, and humiliation and raised to the summit of fame—was good as well as great. His life is proof that there is no depth of human misery from which we may not, by virtue, energy, perseverance, rise to earthly honors, and by God's grace attain eternal glory.

Boys of Grit Vol. I, II, and III

In these volumes of *Boys of Grit*, you will find inspiring true stories like that of an ordinary blacksmith who was able to master twenty languages because he learned to value every spare moment. The life stories of these men will give any boy or girl hope, courage, and the motivation to become all that God desires them to be.

The White Knights W.E. CULE

Three boys in the White Knights Club take on the challenge in their day-to-day lives, just like the knights of King Arthur's court, to prove their faith by their works—protecting "damsels in distress," defending the weak, and honoring their God and King. This story will powerfully change the lives of many young people—forever!

Helen's Temper MRS. GEORGE GLADSTONE

Unlike her tender-hearted sister, Helen's choices are dictated by fear of what her friends might think if she associates with a girl who is so shabby…so different! Her unchecked temper causes great harm, but God's love proves to be greater than she ever imagined.

The Hidden Hand Mrs. E.D.E.N. Southworth

Reader BEWARE—this is NOT your typical Rare Collector book! Strewn with mystery and suspense that never lets up, *The Hidden Hand* will keep you on the edge of your seat! There are not too many books that cause me to laugh aloud (even when I'm alone!). Truly laughter is like medicine, giving health to the bones! But please don't let the feisty, mischievous character of 17-year-old Capitola and the cantankerous personality of Old Hurricane derail you from seeing the gracious providence of an all-wise God. (For ages 16 and up.)

The Mansion Henry van Dyke

This little book is a powerhouse, sending a quickening jolt to the very depths of our respectable-looking façade. *The Mansion* takes a piercing look at John Weightman, one of the most "successful" men in New York, and his son, who desperately wants to find his way and be free to make his own mistakes rather than being played like pieces in a game of chess. *The Mansion*…it will make you think.

Buried in the Snow Franz Hoffman

Full of twists, turns and unexpected dangers, this book will cause you to see life from a different perspective. You will be blessed by the gentle wisdom of an old grandfather and the unconditional love of his grandson as they come face to face with one of the most difficult decisions of their lives. From the depths of despair to the pinnacle of blessing, this dramatic encounter will surely elicit a full spectrum of emotional responses.

True Stories of Great Americans for Young Americans
Anonymous

First published in 1898, this single volume is packed with seldom-heard incidents from the lives of twenty-two great American role models, including Washington, Franklin, Lincoln, Lee, Grant, Garfield, Fulton, Edison, Alcott, Madison, and more. It depicts their natures and habits as young people, and relates scores of incidents of their childhood days, trials, and difficulties, and how they came to be great and famous. Every boy or girl who reads this inspiring volume will want to get out and do something in the world!

The Wide, Wide World (Vol. I and II) SUSAN WARNER
In this endearing novel, little Emily, upon separation from her mother, faces times of unrelenting affliction and heartsickness. But amidst her many disappointments and fears, Emily is pleasantly reminded of the One who has charge over her. This is the very book that "Jo" of Little Women was sobbing over! *The Wide, Wide World* is the first book by an American author to sell one million copies.

The Captive CHRISTOPH VON SCHMID
This gripping account of a kidnapped sixteen-year-old boy will keep you on the edge of your seat! Bought by a rich Muslim family, a powerful drama unfolds as he is faced with a decision that could grant him his freedom—or possibly their freedom in Christ.

A Peep Behind the Scenes MRS. O. F. WALTON
As Rosalie performs on stage the same monotonous acts, the young girls of the village gaze at her with the eyes of admiration and envy. They are certain her life is much more exciting than theirs as they admire her flowing white dress and watch her dance gracefully across the stage. But they do not see what goes on behind the scenes! One day, Rosalie is given hope when an old man gives her a picture of a shepherd who loves her. As she meets hurting people along the way, her new mission is to tell them about the Shepherd who loves them too! Published in 1877, this book sold over 2 and a half million copies!

House of Love ELIZABETH CHENEY
Aurelia Wilde is cruelly selfish and downright miserable—a victim of her mother's desperate attempts to place her delicate "prized possession" on an unreachable pedestal. But her glory is only surface deep. Aurelia's ungrateful, complaining spirit is a stark contrast to that of her servant-girl, Doris, who is convinced that in spite of life's troubles, she will one day "dwell in the house of the Lord forever." She knows that God is Love, and the "house of the Lord" must be the House of Love. Her many talents and her cheerful disposition cause her to be loved and appreciated, even by the notable residents of Waverly Manor. How jealousy swells within Aurelia's vengeful mother! She'll get even yet…

Sir Knight of the Splendid Way W.E. CULE

Sir Knight of the Splendid Way is a captivating allegory—a rich literary masterpiece that will encourage any weary traveler. This beautifully bound work depicts life as a journey, reaching toward a beacon of hope in the City of the Great King. Beckoned by the King to travel the Splendid Way, the young knight must keep his armor on at all cost. All along the way he is challenged and tempted to take his armor off. Many try to convince him that the battle is not worth the fight. Only those who keep their armor on are able to see the real battle that rages before them, and only those with pure hearts will keep their armor on.

The Boy Who Never Lost A Chance ANNETTE LYSTER

Roger Read has learned from his grandfather never to miss a "chance." His hard work, honesty, and diligence are richly rewarded. But having become self-absorbed in his own pursuits, Roger finally realizes something is missing in his life, and he can't seem to find it – until his true friend Jack Sparling helps him to see the best "chance" of all! If you want to inspire your children with an entrepreneurial spirit, balanced with service for God, this is a must-read!

Shipwrecked, But Not Lost HON. MRS. DUNDAS

Impulsive, impatient young boys find themselves reaping the dreadful consequences of following foolish counsel. Stranded in the Artic for the long winter, the two unfortunate lads learn to trust our merciful God as they try to survive against all odds, fighting bears, wolves, and frigid temperatures.

The Basket of Flowers CHRISTOPH VON SCHMID

This first book of the Lamplighter *Rare Collector's Series* continues to be a best-seller. James, the king's gardener, teaches his 15-year-old daughter Mary all the principles of godliness through his flowers. She is falsely accused of stealing, and the penalty is death. Mary remembers her father had taught her that it is better to die for the truth than to live for a lie, and that the worst pillow to sleep on is the pillow of a guilty conscience! This story will change your life forever!

Stepping Heavenward E. PRENTISS

Elisabeth Elliot, Joni Eareckson Tada, and Kay Arthur say that this 19th century book changed their lives. It is an intimate journal—a spiritual journey that will challenge and encourage today's women who long to draw closer to their Savior.

Nobody Loves Me MRS. O. F. WALTON

The neighborhood children call her "Old Grumpy." She is a thin, bony old woman with a hard and cross face, and insists that she loves nobody and nobody loves her. But the day comes when Old Grumpy begins to love and care for an orphaned child like herself. Through this relationship she finally understands the wonderful love of Jesus, who lights up her darkened heart with the sunshine of His love.

LAMPLIGHTER Publishing

BUILDING CHARACTER, ONE STORY AT A TIME.

A DIVISION OF CORNERSTONE FAMILY MINISTRIES

To order a catalog, call us toll free at 1-888-246-7735, email us at mail@lamplighterpublishing.com, or visit our website at www.lamplighterpublishing.com.